What I Wish You Knew

An Addict's Story

Scott King

ISBN (Paperback): 979-8-9996082-1-5

Library of Congress Control Number: 2025915679

This is a work of nonfiction. The events described are based on the author's personal experiences and perspectives. Names and identifying details may have been changed to protect individuals' privacy.

Cover design by Scott King
Published by Scott King
Printed in the United States of America

First Edition

For information, contact:
scotty99099@gmail.com

10 9 8 7 6 5 4 3 2 1

This book is dedicated to my mom and dad, the first people who never gave up on me.

Table of Contents

Intro: So, why are we here? 1

Chapter 1: Where do we start? What is addiction?............. 4

Chapter 2: Where does addiction start? 11

Chapter 3: Let me give you some examples 17

Chapter 4: She learned it from me...........................24

Chapter 5: Another example, and more of my story...........29

Chapter 6: How does addiction really start? 35

Chapter 7: Back to MY story for a minute. 48

Chapter 8: Getting sober isn't easy...........................54

Chapter 9: Living the life! 62

Chapter 10: The manipulation game...........................76

Chapter 11: Helping isn't really helping... 97

Chapter 12: Rehab 108

Chapter 13: So, who am I hurting?........................118

Chapter 14: So now I know who I was hurting..................130

Chapter 15: Destination: Rock Bottom 136

Chapter 16: Another long journey began.....................147

Chapter 17: Time for some hard truth.........................161

Chapter 18: A few words for an addict 164

Chapter 19: So, how do you help an addict? 182

Chapter 20: The guilt and the fear.................................. 224

Chapter 21: Now, the rest of my story............................ 233

Chapter 22: What I Wish You Knew................................. 252

Intro: So, why are we here?

Let's start off by answering a question that will probably be asked by many. I'm not a doctor. I have no medical training or background. I don't come from a family of medical professionals or teachers. I don't have any education in psychology, pharmaceuticals, or anything else related to the healthcare field or industry. I am someone with a past. Some of it good, some of it bad. I'm a father. Some of that role I did as well as I could, some I failed. Other roles that I have had are husband, son, brother, and friend. I have been both good and bad in those roles as well. I am not perfect by any definition. I am a Christian, but I have definitely sinned and fallen short of the glory of God. I am not a CEO of any major corporation. I am just a man who has made mistakes as I traveled this road of life and have learned a few things along the way. Some of the lessons were easy, and I was able to have some successes. Others were very difficult and painful, most learned as I watched those successes slip out of my reach. I am not homeless, but I have been. I am not a rich man and never have been.

I will share some of my experiences in this rambling narrative and hope that someone will gain some understanding, some direction, or some help along the way. My story is my own, but I don't think that it's unique. I know the things my family and friends went through are not unique. I won't make excuses for the things I've done, nor will I allow anyone else to make excuses for me. I will simply tell you my story and, through the words, hope that some can find something that they were searching for. I am not, and have never pretended to be, better or smarter than anyone else. I, like every other person who has ever lived, have a perspective, understanding, and experience that is somewhat unique because we are all different. I faced my challenges and, like most people, had some setbacks. Some of them were out of my control, but most were results of my own choices.

That was a hard realization. That I really didn't know everything. That I really didn't have the life experience, in my younger days, to understand and process everything that I was doing. My parents raised me to know that there were consequences for my actions. It took me many years and mistakes to finally realize that everything I did, everything I had, and everything I had lost were the results of choices I had made. It was a hard, painful realization. But it was probably the best thing that ever happened in my life.

I will share my story and experiences, along with opinions and observations. I will share some stories that involve others so that I can fully tell the story that needs to be told. I will let you get to know me in the hope that I can help someone get through challenges, possibly avoid mistakes, and become the best person that they can be. Again, I am not a medical professional of any kind. I am not trying to sell you any snake oil or any miracles. I am simply telling you what I went through and hope that you can relate and use my story to make yours better. I hope I can prevent someone from making mistakes I've already made.

So, who am I?

I'm an addict.

Chapter 1: Where do we start?

What is addiction?

What is addiction? If you search the Internet, you will find many definitions. Oxford Languages defines addiction as "the fact or condition of being addicted to a particular substance, thing, or activity." That alone isn't really helpful. I have an understanding of addiction based on my experiences. I have been asked when I became addicted to drugs. I can't answer that question. Was it the first time I tried a drug? The tenth, the hundredth? I can't answer that question because I did not realize I was addicted until I was addicted, and by then it was too late.

People can become addicted to many things. Most often, it is associated with drug abuse. But it also includes alcohol, gambling, sex, spending money, and pretty much anything you can think of. A compulsion to use a substance, engage in an activity, or participate in behaviors that consume and control a person is addiction. Continuing the behaviors without the ability to stop, even if it feels or seems harmless, is dangerous. Any addiction can lead to problems with family, friends, employment, and can also lead to health and physical problems. Identifying addiction, and the behaviors associated with addiction, can be difficult. It is also hard, in some cases, to see the behaviors. We don't want to think that someone we care about is addicted to anything. We don't want them to feel hurt or that we are judging them. We don't want to make them feel like we are trying to control them.

I do believe that addiction is a life-long condition. In my opinion, addiction is not something that can be easily defined or summed up in a few words. Addiction is a disease. Like other diseases, it can be treated and overcome. Unlike most diseases, however, addiction takes on many disguises and lives in the shadows. Addiction is often hard to identify, because the addict will try to do everything they can to keep it hidden. Unlike some diseases, addiction can never be fully cured or removed. It can be beaten. It can be overcome. But it never goes away.

I have seen many television commercials, heard many on radio, and read accounts where the statement "I used to be an addict" was used. I disagree with that statement on every level and can never be convinced that it is a true statement. I have never said, and I never will say, "I used to be a drug addict." I AM a drug addict. But I am NOT a drug user. That might seem like a minor distinction, simply another way to say the same thing. But it is not. There is a world of difference.

I have been asked how and when I became addicted to drugs. I have spent many hours over many years trying to find the answer. But the answer is elusive. The truth is, I don't know. I've researched and read many things about addiction. And none of them answered that question. I've found many definitions of addiction, many sources that attempt to describe how addiction starts. Most of them were full of information and details that described what is happening in the brain, what triggers someone to start using a substance, or engaging in a behavior. But not one single thing that I have read or been told answered the question of how and why I became addicted. Medically, yes, the question was answered. I took a substance that increased the dopamine in my brain, I found enjoyment, and I wanted to do it again. While those are all true statements, it is a general answer that doesn't address ME.

I don't pretend to know more than the doctors at some of the best medical facilities in the world. But I do know something that none of them know. I know that I can't answer the question of how or why I became addicted. I have seen many people become frustrated with an addict because they want answers that can't be given. The frustration comes from a desire to help, to understand, and to see someone they care about overcome their addiction. The addict can't answer their questions, so both become frustrated. It is neither one's fault. But it often leads to anger, hurt, and pulling away. The person trying to help has never experienced addiction. They might have been drunk many times but have always been able to leave it and not experience the cravings or compulsion to do it again. They might have smoked a joint once, or many times, and never touched it again. They might have been injured or had surgery and taken opiate pain pills afterwards, but did not become addicted. So, they can't understand how the addict feels that they have no choice but to take a substance, drink alcohol, or participate in a behavior. To me, that is what makes defining addiction so difficult. It has so many variations, so many different faces, that it is different in everyone. From things I have been told and have read, some people believe that addiction can be defined easily and that it should be simple to overcome. Without having been addicted to something, they don't understand.

I was asked by someone who had never experienced addiction, someone who had never felt the cravings, the compulsion to engage in their addiction, or the fear that if they didn't that they would die. I tried to explain it in a way that someone who had never felt those things could relate to. The way I described it is this. Hold your breath. Take in the biggest breath you can and hold it. When you start to see stars, the world starts to darken, and you feel like you'll die if you don't take a breath, don't breathe. If you're holding your breath, you can't help but take that breath. It's not even a choice. You must take that breath, or you will lose consciousness, maybe die. So, you will breathe. An addict feels that same fear when they are without their substance or behavior. The fear is real to them. The fear that they will suffer, possibly die, is real to them. It isn't rational or logical. To anyone else, it wouldn't appear that way. But to the addict that is without their "fix," the fear and compulsion is absolutely real.

When someone tells an addict, "Don't take that drug," "don't take that drink," or "don't do that," the addict only hears "don't take that breath." The addict is feeling the compulsion that anyone would feel to do the only thing that will save them. Inhale. The fact that it isn't rational doesn't matter. The only thing that matters is taking that breath. Cravings and compulsion to use drugs, drink alcohol, place a bet, or any other addictive behavior are very real. They often convince or force the addict to get their "fix."

Stopping, while necessary, can be dangerous for the addict. Quitting "cold turkey" can lead to many physical and emotional problems. It CAN be fatal. People detoxing from drugs or alcohol can become sick, experience mental episodes, behave in unusual, harmful, and unhealthy ways. Some can stop without professional help. But some cannot. While I am not a doctor, I recommend that before you try to stop whatever the addiction is, you consult a medical professional or multiple medical professionals. There are many reputable doctors and facilities that will give you the advice you need, review the situation, and help create a plan that will safely bring the addict to sobriety. Please, please, please don't try this alone. It can be done, but it is not safe. I have lived through detoxing from hard drugs and can't stress enough how bad the pain, both physical and mental, the sickness I suffered for weeks, the emotional strain was for me. And not only for me, but for my family and friends that had to watch me go through it. Again, please seek advice and assistance. For their sake. And yours.

Chapter 2: Where does addiction start?

I've read a lot about addiction. I've talked to a lot of people about it. I've heard a lot of answers and speculation about how addiction happens and how it starts. What do I think? I don't think anyone really knows. I know I can't answer those questions about myself. And every addict I've ever talked to couldn't answer it either. Many things can lead to addiction. If addiction had an identifiable cause, origin, or starting point, it would have been identified long ago. But it is different for everyone and, therefore, can't be so easily defined.

Many factors can be involved in addiction. Some feel that environment and challenges we face in our early lives lead to addiction. While it can have an impact, our childhood and early lives can't be made a scapegoat for choices that we ultimately make. Some face adversity and turn to alcohol or drugs as an escape, while others who face the same challenges go in the opposite direction. It all comes down to how we cope, what we want for our lives, and the choices we make.

Some addicts come from a family and background of love and stability. Having a family that isn't "broken," where Mom and Dad get married, build the "perfect" life, and have children that they raise with love and attention, doesn't guarantee that a person won't become addicted to something. Even when the parents don't consume alcohol or drugs, never display negative behaviors, and work to nurture and teach their children, choices can lead us down a path that shouldn't have been possible. As we grow up, meet people, and have more life experiences, we are often in situations where the choices we make determine our futures. Even when we don't realize it. "Good" kids can allow themselves to be diverted from the path their parents were leading them to by many things. Curiosity, peer pressure, culture, television, movies, and many other things can introduce behaviors that will lead to problems in our futures.

Some people, sadly, have parents, family members, or friends that lead with bad examples. If a child grows up in an environment where bad behaviors are seen and are part of "normal, everyday life," they could believe that these things are normal and acceptable. If we see the authority figures in our lives drinking, taking drugs, engaging in other negative behaviors, we become desensitized and can start to believe that is how life is supposed to be. Watching the people we love, and who should be nurturing and teaching us, participate in negative, self-destructive behaviors can result in teaching us that it is perfectly fine and normal to live this way.

Others become addicted because of accidents and injuries. If someone is hurt, they can be prescribed narcotic pain medications intended to help. If the medicines are not taken as prescribed, and even sometimes when they are, or taken for an extended period, a person can become dependent, addicted, to them. Many doctors over many years prescribed narcotic pain killers too freely. Maybe in the early years, doctors didn't fully understand the danger of extended use, maybe they did, but didn't care. Either way, pharmaceutical companies, pain clinics, and pill mills continued to push narcotics and create drug addicts. In many cases, the pills started to lose their effectiveness, and the person turned to other drugs to get the relief they were seeking. Sometimes doctors stopped prescribing the pain medication, and the person had to find a substitute for that relief. The original goal was not to become addicted to a drug, but the addiction happened.

Many medical professionals believe that some people are more likely to become addicts because of genetics. Some people can't metabolize substances and are more affected by alcohol or drugs. Studies have been done to identify the parts of the brain that cause and are affected by addiction. Some have claimed that they have located these areas and causes. But addiction still happens. If a solution or cure had really been found, addiction would have been eradicated.

I believe that addiction is a combination of many things. Some physiological, some psychological. Some are environmental, some learned. But the combination that leads to addiction is different for everyone. Addiction is a disease that, as I have stated before, has many faces and is a very manipulative, sneaky thing. Because of the infinite number of possibilities, addiction is a disease unlike any other.

Addiction can't be summed up easily, it can't be simply handled. Addiction is a living thing, in my opinion, and must be experienced to be fully understood. Without living in addiction, it is probably impossible to fully comprehend what the addict experiences. The cravings, the uncontrollable urge to partake or behave in a certain way, to fear what will happen if we don't. These are things that can't be learned from a book or watching people in a study. These feelings must be lived, experienced, and FELT to really be understood.

Many professionals, doctors, and facilities are available to help the addict get sober. And many of them do a great job of helping people change their lives. They can help addicts identify their triggers, their weakness, and to find new ways to respond to life's challenges without drinking alcohol, doing drugs, or engaging in self-destructive behaviors. Many addicts can achieve sobriety with help from these institutions and professionals. But to achieve success and sobriety, the addict must want it. Only the addict can truly fix themselves.

One thing that leads to addiction that is always present is choice. Choices we make, behaviors we participate in, for enjoyment or escape, affect our lives and our futures. We can be nurtured and taught to make good choices, we can be neglected and left to learn on our own. But in the end, we make choices. Good, bad, right or wrong. We make choices. And we must live with the consequences of those choices, good or bad.

So, where does addiction come from and how does it start? While that question cannot ever be fully, definitively answered, CHOICE is always a part. We made a choice to take that first drink, use a drug for the first time, engage in bad behavior. Our outcome could have been different if we had made a different, better choice. While a "cure" for addiction will probably never be found or developed, a way to save an addict is to help them choose to make better choices.

Chapter 3: Let me give you some examples

I was raised by the best people that I have ever known. My parents were married for 56 years, so obviously I'm not from a broken home. My parents were small business owners. We weren't rich, but we didn't do without. I grew up in a middle-class home with parents that were caring and engaged in my life. I was raised in a Christian home. We attended church regularly. My dad was a deacon, taught Sunday School, and my mom played piano for the church. My parents didn't drink and never did any kind of illegal drugs. I was taught that those activities and behaviors were wrong and that I should never start doing either. Before starting their small business, my dad was a schoolteacher and principal. My aunt was a schoolteacher as well. Education was a very big priority growing up. I couldn't have asked for a more loving, attentive, or stable childhood.

I was injured in a motorcycle accident when I was in middle school. I broke my leg in several places and spent a little time in the hospital as a result. While I was in the hospital, I was introduced to narcotic pain medicine. I had to have knee surgery about six weeks after the accident because the breaks in my knee were growing together out of alignment. I was given more narcotics, opiate pain medication. I was never given more than the prescribed doses, and the medications were stopped as soon as I didn't need them anymore. I didn't have any withdrawal symptoms that I can remember, and eventually healed and went on with my life. But my body had been introduced to opiates.

I, like my mom, played piano. During my sophomore year in high school, I entered a talent show. After the talent show, a few older students asked if I would join their band. They were seniors, two years older than I was. I joined them and we spent a lot of time together, playing music and just hanging out. They smoked marijuana. I had never been around it, but I was very curious. They did not try to get me to join them, and refused to let me when I asked. They said no many times. But I was still curious and never stopped asking. They eventually let me join them, and I, I am sad to say, liked it.

That band didn't last very long because two of the members were seniors and left for college that fall. But it didn't end my use of marijuana. I went to college and quickly discovered that many others shared my enthusiasm for it, and it was a regular part of our college life. During my freshman year at college, I discovered other drugs and experimented a lot. Like my introduction to marijuana, no one pressured me, enticed me, or even asked me to try different drugs. I was curious, as I have always been, and always asked to try whatever was available.

I left college after one year because I wasn't interested in continuing my education. I went back to my hometown and started working. I moved out of my parents' house and, with a friend, got an apartment. Our apartment quickly became the party pad for all of our friends. We would spend our off days drinking, smoking pot, and generally being irresponsible teens. We were 19 and thought that we knew everything. We kept the apartment for almost one year. My roommate, who had also gone to college for one year and stopped, entered the military. He had never tried the drugs with me or anyone else. He drank alcohol, we all did. After he left, my family helped me get an old mobile home and put it on my parents' property. It was isolated and in what had been a pasture. It became the party house. I continued working, playing music, and, of course, doing various drugs. I would do drugs for a while, then stop for a long time. I wasn't addicted then and could start then stop without any cravings or problems.

I eventually met the girl who would become my first wife. We had two daughters. We drank alcohol, but we did not do drugs. Eventually, we made new friends, and I started smoking marijuana again with some of them. That marriage, after a few years, came to an end.

My daughters lived with me. I had stopped playing in bands when they were born, but started again after the divorce. And alcohol and marijuana were once again a big part of it. I met new people, and through them, found new drugs to try.

I started taking opiate pain pills after suffering a back injury. I got through that period and stopped the pills, as I had stopped after my broken leg. I later reinjured my back and took more pain pills. That time I didn't stop. I had discovered that they sped me up, and I liked that effect. I continued to take pain pills – hydrocodone, Percocet, oxycontin – and would get them wherever and however I could. When it took several pills to get what I wanted, I moved on to harder, more powerful drugs.

I was, I'm not proud to say, very irresponsible in many ways. My daughters were, by then, in their early teens. I didn't hide what I was doing, the drinking, partying, and doing drugs. I didn't give them any. But I allowed them to know what I was doing and see what I was doing. Like I said, I failed as a father.

Time, as it has a way of doing, moved on, and I met my second wife. She was also a drug user. I didn't realize what was happening because I spent so much time under the influence of one drug or another. What I failed to see was that for a long time, I had been behaving in a way that told my daughters that using drugs and not being responsible was acceptable. I got my first and only DUI, but still didn't learn. And I didn't stop using drugs.

My second marriage was very toxic and didn't last too long. Near the end, one of my daughters was caught with marijuana and pills at school. She was arrested. I was still waiting for my court date for the DUI. I went to the courthouse the day my daughter was to be sentenced. My family knew the judge, and he decided to challenge me. He asked if I could handle my daughter if he released her to me. I said that I could. He said, and I will remember these words for the rest of my life, "Maybe it will do you both some good."

That statement hit me hard. Very hard. He released her then and there. He had the bailiff remove her shackles and allowed her to leave with me. I told her that day that we both had to get ourselves clean and start living the life we should. It wasn't easy, and it wasn't that simple. I stumbled through getting clean, and she did too. For a while.

I had lost everything. I had built a house. I had vehicles. I had musical equipment. But living the life of a drug user, I sold or lost all of it over time. The day my daughter was released from the courthouse, I was practically homeless. I had a hand-me-down minivan, enough clothes to fill maybe half of a small closet, and nothing else. But I had a new purpose. And a new understanding of just how bad a father, role model, and person I had been. I finally realized that I had been instrumental in my daughter becoming a drug user and the destruction of my previous marriages and life. I had made many really disastrous choices in my life and knew that I had to make the most import ones of all to get it right.

I will come back to this point a little later. Now I want to share a few other examples of different circumstances that show different paths to addiction. I have talked to the people in these stories and have their permission to include them here. While you might wonder if these stories are made up, I assure you that they are real. And they are all people that I know, people that I love. I don't need to go beyond my own family and friends to find varied stories of addiction and the problems that follow it. Because addiction is something that is too easily found in too many lives.

Chapter 4: She learned it from me

My daughter and I got our lives together for a while. I met my third wife, and we moved in together. My daughter was still a minor and lived with us. I had managed to get clean and stay that way. My daughter lived with us for a few months. We lived in a different county, and she had started a new school. We were still close to where we had lived before, so she was still in contact and spending time with some of her old friends.

We had a few setbacks during those months. She had started taking pills and had some at our home. She dropped one, and my wife found it on the floor. That caused a situation that could have jeopardized everything. My relationship with my then girlfriend, my sobriety, the puppy that my daughter had wanted.

My daughter had made the choice to return to some of her previous behaviors. She didn't want to go to school. She didn't want to help around the house. She had her mother sign papers and allow her to quit school.

While I was never a perfect father, I had some rules. One of which was high school graduation was not optional. My parents had the same rule. If you don't graduate from high school, you can't live in our house. My daughter went to live with her mother that day. After moving, she reconnected with some of her old friends and drug buddies and returned to her old ways. She, like I had done years before, thought that she was having fun and that she wasn't hurting anyone. She met a boy, and they had a child. Both were still using drugs, and the child was taken from them. They broke up. He ended up going to prison. My daughter moved around, living friend to friend and couch to couch. Still using drugs and caught up in that life. Her son, my grandson, was in the foster system. He was ultimately taken permanently and was adopted by another family.

My daughter was devastated. Instead of letting this be her wakeup call, she sank deeper into her addiction. She started using more powerful drugs and using more often. She overdosed at least two times and had to be saved by EMTs with Narcan. She was arrested on more than one occasion and spent days and weeks in jail. Somewhere along her journey she reconnected with a young man that she had gone to school with. His story is another one that I will share, but will skip ahead to finish telling hers. They started a relationship, but he had a problem with her drinking and drug use. He told her that he wouldn't be with her unless she stopped all her bad behavior. She had lost her son, her family, and was about to lose him too.

That was her wakeup call. She found a rehab that was a six-month program. It started off as a lock down program. Her phone was taken, she wasn't allowed to have any visitation. She was only allowed to use the phone in the office, under supervision, and for very limited amounts of time. She was required to attend meetings and counseling. It was very hard for her to do this. She had to detox, had never been in a position where she was locked down, and her entire life monitored and controlled. She thought many times of leaving. She could have, as the program was voluntary, and she had entered on her own. But she didn't.

After the first few weeks, she was allowed visits. The visitations were in the office and supervised. The visitors were not allowed to see where she came from, know which building or room she lived in, and had to be on an approved list. The visits were timed and limited to a small number of people. After a few more weeks of this, she earned the privilege of unsupervised, off-site visits. These visits were still timed and limited to only approved people.

After the first few months, she was required to get a job and save her money so that when she completed the program, she would have something to start her new life. The young man who had forced her to face herself and her addiction had kept his word. He was waiting for her. She completed the full program, graduated from the program, and they began a new life together. She was contacted by the family that had adopted her son. She was told that she could see him, have contact with him, and be part of his life if she remained drug free. She was not expecting the offer but gladly accepted the opportunity and the rules that accompanied. We had all been out of his life for a long time. We all missed him. And we were all happy to have the chance to get to know him, watch him grow, and share part of his life.

My daughter, at the time I am writing this, has been clean for over two years. That might seem like a long time to anyone who has never been trapped in addiction. She still has a long road ahead, but is making better choices and traveling in a better direction.

The young man that delivered my daughter's wakeup call had his own demons in his past. He had been a drug user, an addict, and had gotten caught up in a situation that landed him in prison. He served one year and got clean while he was there. He came out a changed, better person. He had seen the mistakes and was determined not to repeat them. He reconnected with my daughter and, while he loved her, wasn't willing to be with someone who wouldn't stop the self-destructive behaviors. He gave her an ultimatum, and, by some miracle, she listened. I knew him briefly when he was using drugs and still making the wrong choices. We didn't get along then.

They, the young man and my daughter, have been building a better life together for the past two years. He is a part of her son's life, as she is, and they have come to help each other stay focused on their future. To make better choices and not slide back into the wrong kind of life. They have both earned my respect.

Chapter 5: Another example, and more of my story

I met my third wife during a very difficult part of my life. I was still working on myself. I was clean, but I was still fighting to stay that way. I had been drug-free for almost one year. I was still feeling and fighting the cravings. She had been married before, also. Her first husband had passed away a few years before we met. She had had a good marriage, but not one without its own problems. She shared her history and laid down some rules that were non-negotiable. Her husband had been an alcoholic. By all accounts, a good man, good father, but, like all of us, with his own flaws and demons. She told me that she would not be with someone who used drugs, abused alcohol, or exhibited any negative or self-destructive behavior.

We lived together for a long time before getting married. She was cautious, and rightly so, and wanted to make sure that she was not re-entering a relationship with a shadow that could ruin it. I was still fighting my demons, too. She supported me, helped me to stay focused, and ultimately to win my battles and return to who I was supposed to be.

My wife had two sons from her first marriage. One was responsible, had a wife, and a direction in his life that he would not allow to be diverted. He and his wife are both very driven and successful. They have a daughter and a very stable life and future.

Her youngest son, sadly, didn't follow the same path. He had seen his father drinking alcohol and discovered it for himself as a teenager. As many teenagers do, he had friends and enjoyed the party life. What he also had, that he didn't know, was the inability to metabolize alcohol. And he became addicted quickly. He had started down a path that would bring him problems, instability, and heartache.

He married young, and he and his wife had a son. Their life was not easy, as he never stopped drinking and frequently lost or changed jobs. As is the case with most addicts, he worked where he could continue drinking and get by as long as he could. His marriage lasted several years but eventually fell apart.

He was diagnosed with cirrhosis. He was hospitalized and was in very bad shape, and very nearly died. He was in the hospital for many days and eventually started to recover. The first time he was hospitalized he was jaundiced, his liver was failing, ammonia was attacking his brain, and we didn't know if he could survive. By some miracle, he recovered enough to be released from the hospital. He tried to stop drinking but was not successful. He lived with friends, continued to make bad choices, and eventually landed back in the hospital. He again managed to get better and moved into his brother's home. He tried again to give up alcohol. He stayed at his brother's home for six months, but started sneaking alcohol again. He left his brother's home and moved back to where he had spent most of his youth.

He found a job and lived in an extended stay hotel. He told everyone that he was sober and doing better. That he was on his way to a sober life. His son moved in with him, and everything seemed to be on the right track. Until it wasn't.

He reconnected with old friends and slid back into old habits. He lost his job and place to live. His son ultimately had to move back to live with his mother. He moved in with friends and continued to abuse alcohol.

The party life didn't last long, as his friends, who also drank alcohol and enjoyed the party life, had real world responsibilities. They worked, had bills to pay, and their homes to maintain. He stayed drunk and unable, or unwilling, to work and was eventually told to leave. He went through more than one friend and couch.

He had spent many years manipulating family and friends. He had been given money, had his bills paid, rent paid, food provided, and places to stay by many people. He would lose his job and ask for help. Many people tried, but weren't really helping. They were enabling. Because no one wanted to see him suffer, or homeless, we would give in and provide the means to continue his bad behavior. We would all try to talk to him, get him to stop drinking alcohol, get and keep a job, but it never lasted. He was in and out of hospitals, never accepting that his choices were the root of and continuation of his problems.

Eventually, it reached a point where no one was willing or able to help financially anymore. He went to a homeless shelter. A place that was supposed to give people a place to live while they got their lives under control. They did not provide any rehab services, counseling, or help with addiction. They did not allow the use of drugs or alcohol while staying at their facility, and monitored and tested the residents. He was eventually caught, failed a breathalyzer test, and was told he had to leave. As had happened before, he told a story that left out that part. He tried to convince everyone that he had been following the rules, and that the facility had been caught doing wrong and was being closed. He asked that someone, anyone, allow him to live with them or "loan" him money to get a place of his own. When no one would do either, he entered a rehab program.

He had a problem with the rehab and left. He couch-surfed again for a few weeks until he was again told he had to leave. He attempted to force his way into a family member's home. When that attempt failed, he went to the hospital again and had the advocate help him find another detox facility. He went, and soon after began to have problems with that facility. He found a rehab and was transferred there. He completed the initial program and received a Certificate of Completion. He left the rehab and once again found a motel that offered extended stay rates.

Less than two weeks after leaving rehab, he faced some adversity and once again turned to alcohol to escape. He again went to the hospital seeking "help." He was placed in a behavioral and addiction detox facility. If family members had not gone to the motel, he would have lost the few belongings he still had. He was out of money and out of time and was going to be checked out of the motel while he was at the hospital. While at the detox facility, he had the staff contact family in an attempt to return to someone's home. Again, the family had to refuse.

He continued to try to get someone, anyone, to come and get him out of the detox facility, but no one did. He had no choice but to enter yet another rehab and, at the time of this writing, is still there, in his first week.

He has been supported by family and friends. He has received emotional and financial support from many people. But everyone who has "helped" has reached a point where we can't help anymore. This cycle of "getting sober," failing, ending up in a hospital, going to rehab, then starting the whole cycle over again has been ongoing for over four years. The stories change. The details are slightly different. But in the end, nothing has changed. His family and friends are stuck waiting to see if this time is real. Or just another restart for failure.

Chapter 6: How does addiction really start?

The examples presented are all real. The stories have been condensed, but show a brief look at different scenarios, the influences, and results. The point? All addiction stories are different, so they must all be faced differently. None of the stories completely answer the question "how does addiction start," but they offer insight that can help understand how and why it does.

My personal journey started through curiosity. And injury. But I do not blame my injuries or the doctors that gave me pain meds to help me get through them for my later addiction. I could easily tell you that because I was introduced to opiate pain medications that I became addicted. I don't deny that having been slowly introduced through multiple injuries and rounds of narcotic pain pills made it easier for me, but I can't say that those things led to or really had anything to do with my becoming addicted later in my life.

While I still can't give a complete, definitive answer to the question, I can give an educated, experienced opinion. But that is not all of it. Other factors were involved that led to me being dependent on drugs. Choices that I made, reasonable or not, were the biggest factor.

I, like many others, went to parties, had friends, and wanted to have fun. It is natural for humans to seek enjoyment, pleasure, and to have a desire to explore and experience new things. Some people like to jump out of airplanes. Some like to race cars. Some like to climb mountains or explore caves. Some people are extroverted and have no problem being the "life of the party," making friends, or fitting in in a group. Others, many people, do have a problem doing those things. Many people feel that they are "not enough," or lack something that would make them popular, attractive, or accepted by their peers. Some people that feel that something in them is missing often turn to something else to find it, make it stand out more, or make others see it. Other people use substances or behaviors to enhance themselves, to make their actions and behaviors more visible. Not because they feel they aren't seen. They want to be seen on a larger scale.

Another way that many are exposed to alcohol, drugs, or improper behaviors is peer pressure. Often, a group will tell a person that they can't be included if they don't do something. If they don't smoke this joint, they can't be included. If they don't drink alcohol, they will be left out. If they don't participate in whatever behavior or activity the group is doing, they can't be allowed in. They are forced to make a choice. Even if they know that the decision to drink alcohol, use the drug, or participate in the activity is wrong, they will do it, so they won't be ostracized and left out, excluded. People often make choices that they know are not in their best interests just to be accepted. They are told that they won't be liked, won't be "cool," and will be alone if they don't conform and do what the group wants and does.

Peer pressure isn't just about drinking alcohol or using drugs. It can be anything. It can lead to someone taking dangerous, unnecessary risks while driving or doing other activities. It can lead to someone having sex before they are emotionally ready, or with someone they don't really want to be with. If your friends all want to bet on a ball game and you don't, you could place a bet anyway if they threaten to leave you out if you refuse. Someone could dare you to jump off of a cliff into a creek or lake without knowing what was under the water's surface. It could be drinking alcohol or taking drugs, but it doesn't have to be those specific things. Peer pressure is forcing someone to do something that they don't feel comfortable doing, to get them to act in a certain way, to get them to do something they are afraid of doing or know is wrong. Peer pressure is bullying. It is wrong. But it is part of life, especially when we are young and impressionable, and often leads us places we didn't want to visit.

Other people, like me, are curious. We are always looking for new experiences. We are, in most cases, adrenaline junkies and always try to go faster, reach higher, do more. And when we can't do those things on our own, we look for something to help us get there. Too many times, we mistakenly believe that a drug or something external can help us reach that next level. Then the next, and the next. Sometimes it is just because we see something that we haven't experienced and want to give it a try. We make choices because we want to know, to feel, to experience new things in new ways. We don't always make the best choices or think things through. We just act. Consequences be damned. And we often end up paying a price for the rash choices we make.

Television, movies, books, social media, and other things also often portray bad behaviors as acceptable and fun. We see people drinking, using drugs, engaging in all manner of questionable behavior, and have largely become desensitized to it. We have come to expect to see these things. We have learned, through environment and demonstration, that these activities happen "all the time" and are "normal." Sometimes there are negative consequences, but most of the time all is forgiven and forgotten before the End Credits start to roll. We are shown that whatever we do, however inappropriate or bad for us it is, it all works out in the end. And that there are often no long-term ill effects, no lasting consequences, no permanent damage, and no physical or emotional price to pay. We are misled, partly by the presentation, partly by our own misunderstanding and bias, into failing to see the real damage these things do and the effects they have.

It also happens that people become addicted because we didn't want to see it. We teach our children, as our parents hopefully taught us, that certain things and behaviors are wrong, are bad, and shouldn't be allowed. If we see that someone – a friend, our child, another family member – is exhibiting behaviors that are destructive or harmful to themselves, we often try to make excuses. We don't want to see that someone we care about is abusing drugs or alcohol or engaging in self-destructive behaviors. We try to find ways to explain it in a way that relieves them of guilt and blame. We don't want to see them hurt, or hurt their feelings, or alienate them, so we overlook things. We might even be blind to it, willfully or subconsciously, and refuse to accept what we are seeing and know is happening. We don't want to think that that person is capable of doing things to hurt us, hurt themselves, or participate in anything that they know they shouldn't.

Some addictions have started because someone has been injured, had surgeries, or other health problems that led to doctors prescribing opiate pain medications. They didn't intend to get hurt, get sick, or undergo surgery. But it happened. While going through the aftermath and recovery, they started taking the pills more often than the prescription called for. They would be out of their medication before the scheduled time. I have known people who have been in this situation. They all said the same thing. They said that they needed it to stop the pain. And they all said they didn't have a problem because the pills had been prescribed by their doctor.

I was guilty of this. And I said the same thing. It's got to be ok because the doctor wouldn't have given them to me if I wasn't supposed to take them. I rationalized that what I was doing was acceptable because I was in pain and that a doctor had told me to do it. What I didn't take into consideration was that the doctor had included instructions. How much to take, how often to take it, and the words I never seemed to hear or see, AS NEEDED for the pain. I allowed myself to increase the amount by reducing the time between doses. I unintentionally started abusing opiate pain pills because I thought I was helping myself.

I have known people that suffered from chronic pain and were referred to pain clinics. They were prescribed opiate pain medications and given instructions on their use. Some of the clinics did regular checks, counting pills, checking for drug levels with blood tests, and monitoring the patients. I have also known of clinics that were less attentive to details and did not track these things. Clinics and doctors that just kept prescribing more and more pain pills, increasing their strength and dose, with no regard for the person taking them. I have even heard, personally with my own ears, a pain clinic doctor tell a patient that they WILL become ADDICTED to the pain pills. He said it matter-of-factly, like that was the expected and acceptable outcome. In effect, telling the person that addiction was the price that had to be paid to be pain free.

Some doctors, whether they admit it or not, whether anyone wants to believe it or not, prescribe medications because they receive incentives from pharmaceutical companies. Financial, material, or other things that they want and receive because they continue to present a particular medication or treatment to patients.

In short, many people become addicted to opiate pain medications through legitimate beginnings. They didn't intend to become addicted to opiates. They probably never thought it could happen to them. But it did. And if, when, the prescriptions end, they still have the "need" for it. If they can't get it from a doctor or legitimate source, they often find other ways to get it. Finding friends who have prescriptions that they don't take, borrowing or stealing from someone who has pain medication, or from an unknown source, "the street." Some will do whatever it takes to get what they want. Some will pay, some will exchange something – material goods, sex, or whatever they can – to get their desired outcome. And in many cases, illegal, unsafe, and infinitely more harmful drugs are substituted when the opiate pain pills can't be found or aren't providing the result that was desired.

Depression often leads people to places where addiction is a very real danger, and often the final destination. Other issues – anxiety, PTSD, emotional or physical trauma – can cause this as well. Some become addicted to the medications that are prescribed to help with these problems. Some do not. Some don't find the level of relief that they need and move to other substances to seek that release. Some self-medicate with alcohol, drugs, sex, gambling, or something else. They never meant to abuse anything and become addicted, but they end up trapped just the same. They self-medicate because they are afraid to seek help from others. They could fear that family or friends would judge them, or be hurt in some way, if they admitted their problems. They might feel that they would be seen as weak because they couldn't process and work through whatever problems they were facing. They could feel uncomfortable telling a stranger, a medical professional, or anyone else, their situation. Fear, embarrassment, uncertainty, or simply

43

not knowing where to look or how to ask for help can leave someone feeling they have no alternative to self-medicating.

Many, many times, people will say that they started drinking alcohol, using drugs, or engaging in other questionable and self-destructive behaviors to escape. They have something happen in their life that they can't understand, can't find a way out of, and that makes them feel that they have no options, nowhere to turn. It can be many things. Losing a job, a relationship ending, death of a family member or friend. These things, and countless others, can make a person feel lost, trapped, and lead to depression. When we face adversity, we often look for something to make it go away, to rescue us and take us somewhere better, safer. Somewhere where we don't hurt or suffer. A distraction. Too many times, we are unable to find help, to find an answer, or to find peace. Many people find themselves in this situation and truly believe that the only solution is to run away from it. To drink themselves into forgetting. To use a drug to hide what has happened. Or to engage in other activities or behaviors that make them forget, for a minute, the pain, the sorrow, the situation that they were facing. They use a substance or activity to distract them, to allow them to pretend that the

44

problem isn't there, or to simply run away from the problem and hide. Some people fall fully into addiction while trying to escape adversity. They might have consumed alcohol, used drugs recreationally, or engaged in behaviors that were potentially addictive but had not reached full dependence. But in running to that substance, that act, that thing, they end up losing themselves completely to its control and influence.

This often leads to a relapse for an addict. Getting sober is not an easy task. When a person stops using a substance or a behavior that they are addicted to, the cravings, the need, don't automatically go away. That need, the cravings, the irrational desire to return to a substance or behavior, can be very, very strong and long lasting. When a setback comes, the automatic impulse is to run back to their substance of choice and escape, to hide. For many, addiction and use of substances or participation in behaviors has been a part of their life for many years. They have often spent more time with their addiction than sobriety. Their addiction, their mind, manipulates them to believe that returning to that familiar place will provide protection, escape, from the bad thing. While that is not real, or true, it can be very easy for the addict to believe. Because they have lived much of their lives, in many cases, under the influence of that demon, it is easy to believe the whispered lies.

Many recovering addicts are lost because they are unable to face adversity, unpleasant situations, or even guilt because of their past behaviors. They can feel that they are unforgivable, that they don't deserve or won't get another chance. That no one will believe that they are really trying to escape the claws of their demon. That no help is there. While it might feel like there is no help, no options, there is always a way. Medical professionals, counselors, rehab, and detox facilities are options. They might not make an addict feel good about themselves or their situation, but they can provide the help that is sometimes so desperately needed.

There are many roads that lead to addiction. The early signs are often difficult to see. Whether they are hidden by the person engaging in the activity, people aren't seeing because they don't want to see, the beginning of addiction is often missed. And not realized and accepted until it is too late.

Addiction is different in everyone and presents in so many ways that it is hard to identify. The early warning signs are often misunderstood, ignored, or lost in the chaos of everyday life. Answering the question, "how does someone become addicted," is very difficult, if not impossible. But it is a real concern, and it does happen.

Thankfully, the question doesn't have to be answered to escape addiction, or to help someone find their way back to sobriety. The question shouldn't be "how did you let this happen," "why did you get addicted to this," "why did you start doing that." The question should be "how do we get you back."

Chapter 7: Back to MY story for a minute.

In my story, I saw others smoking a joint and wanted to know what it was. They told me what it was and how it made them feel. I wanted to try it. Not because they invited me to, but because I wanted to experience it for myself. They first told me no, that I shouldn't do it. That I was too young and that it was a bad idea. I didn't accept that and kept asking until they gave in. They, against their initial objections, let me try it. I enjoyed the way it made me feel. I wanted to do more. Experts will say that what I experienced was, possibly, endorphins being released in my brain, or dopamine making me feel that I had achieved something. While that is probably true, I only knew that I liked it and couldn't wait until the next time I could smoke it. I wasn't interested in details, medical facts or theories, proven empirical research, or statistics. I wanted to feel good, and smoking marijuana allowed me to feel good. That was all that mattered to me. The happy feeling I felt when I got high. I didn't see a problem with it, I didn't think I was hurting anyone, and, therefore, saw it as an acceptable activity. So, I didn't stop. I had made several choices. I chose to start. And I chose to continue.

I eventually did stop smoking marijuana. Things and events in my life led me to places where it wasn't accepted, wasn't helpful, and hindered my ability to achieve. I know those things now, looking back many years later. At the time, I just decided to stop. I had moved on with my life and just lost interest. The people I was with, the job that I had, and the life I was living didn't allow me to be who I had been. I got married and became a father. In my mind, husbands and fathers weren't supposed to use drugs, so I didn't. For a while.

I wanted to be a good husband and father. I changed many things about myself and my lifestyle so that I could be both. No one forced me to change. I made a choice to change. I left low paying, no future jobs and tried to find a career, something that would allow me to make more money and better provide for my family. I did that for a few years. Eventually, we met new friends and discovered that some of them smoked marijuana. I felt that I had achieved some of the things I had wanted to do and that I could smoke marijuana occasionally and not suffer for it. My first wife did not participate, but she didn't try to stop me from doing it. I didn't smoke often. I shouldn't have smoked at all.

Many things led to the failure of my first marriage. My smoking marijuana wasn't the main cause, but I'm sure it didn't help. I was single for a few years after my first divorce. My daughters continued to live with me. They had seen very little in their early years, as we were very careful trying to hide our alcohol consumption and my marijuana use from them. After the divorce, I became less diligent, and they started seeing more of my bad behaviors. I started playing music again and, with some friends, formed another garage band.

The band would practice at our house. We drank alcohol, smoked marijuana, and we did it without regard for who was seeing it. We were enjoying playing music, spending time together, and just having fun. It never registered that my young, pre- and early teenage daughters were watching, seeing, and being taught that this was all acceptable. While they were never invited to participate, they were being educated. And they were being taught bad lessons by irresponsible teachers.

I had raised my daughters as my parents had raised me, trying to teach them right from wrong, things they shouldn't do, and behaviors they should avoid. I was telling them to do as I said, not as I did. I was so busy, so preoccupied, with moving on with my life that I failed to see that I was being a hypocrite. That I was telling them, with words, that the things they were seeing me DO, through my actions, were wrong. I was leading them to believe that drinking alcohol and recreational drug use were acceptable. My choices were affecting my girls. I chose to do things that I knew were not good for me, were not acceptable. And I chose to do it where they could see it. Doing it at all was wrong. Letting them see it, teaching them that it was ok, was worse.

My choices quite likely led to helping them make choices of their own. Most of them bad. My experimentation with different, more illicit and harmful drugs, continued, and I got lost in my addiction.

I met my second wife. She used drugs, too, so we were a disaster waiting to happen. That marriage was very toxic. It was unhealthy for me, but more so for my daughters. They were treated unfairly. Most of that part of my life was spent lost to one drug or another, and I didn't pay attention to how it was hurting my daughters. Because of my drug use, inattention, and irresponsibility, I lost everything. We had built a house, bought vehicles, musical equipment, and tools. I lost a very good job and was unable to find anything that was comparable. I eventually lost that house, started selling my equipment and tools. My daughters went to live with my parents. I lived where I could and continued to chase drugs through my downward spiral.

I got away with my lifestyle for a long time. Then I didn't. I was under the influence of a cocktail of drugs and was trying to text and drive. I was swerving badly, and I was stopped by a police officer. I went to jail for DUI. Sadly, I didn't learn a thing. As soon as I was out of jail, I went back to the drugs and self-destructive behaviors. I had a chance to make a better choice, but I chose wrong. Again.

A few weeks after my DUI arrest, my daughter was caught with drugs at school. That part of the story has already been told, and I mention it again to emphasize that it was my wakeup call.

That wakeup call was my rock-bottom. It was my worst moment. And it was painful. But the pain, as I would soon discover, was only beginning. I started getting clean. It took a long time, but I made it. I tried to do it alone, but I couldn't. But my daughter was worth it. I was worth it. And I owed it to her, to me, and to many others – my parents, friends, my other daughter – to try, to fight, to not give up. And to eventually find sobriety.

Chapter 8: Getting sober isn't easy

I have been asked by many people why it's so hard to get sober. To someone who has never been addicted to anything, it is almost impossible to explain in a way that they can relate to. I was told many times that I should just put it down, not do it anymore. I wish it were that simple. But sadly, it is not. It was the hardest task I have ever started in my life. Started. Because it is a task that never ends.

The first step in overcoming addiction is a desire to stop the behavior. I have read many things that describe how an addict can be made to "see the light." There have been television shows that depict a group of people – family, friends, professional medical people, or combinations of all of them – performing interventions. Many people tried countless ways to get me to stop using drugs. And everything they tried failed. It fell on deaf ears. Because I didn't WANT to stop. Everyone who cared about me wanted me to stop. Many of them offered to help, and gave what they thought was help. But it was all wasted effort. I wish I could say that it changed something in me that helped me turn my addiction around. But I would be lying if I said that any of it even made a dent. Because I didn't want to stop.

As you read in Chapter 1, the best comparison I can think of is breathing. It might seem insane to think of that as it relates to addiction, but it is the best comparison I have ever been able to come up with. A person breathes without thought. When we are born, we take our first breath, and we start to cry. And hopefully we don't stop breathing for a very long time. It is natural, it happens without thought. It is automatic. And without breathing, we die. Children sometimes hold their breath in an attempt to get something they want. They threaten to hold their breath forever if their demands are not met. They hold their breath for a period of time, but eventually can't stop themselves from inhaling. They can't control the compulsion to take that breath. Their body doesn't give them a choice. They might be able to hold it long enough to see stars, maybe everything starts to dim, to go dark. They might even briefly lose consciousness. But they will reach a point where they can't resist any longer, and they will breathe. If you doubt the strength of compulsion, try it. Take the deepest breath you can and hold it. Don't inhale when the first impulse comes. Or the second. Fight yourself, your body, your mind as long as you can. You might be able to hold your breath for a long time. Or it might be just seconds. But you WILL reach a point where you can't fight it anymore. And you will take a breath. You won't be able to stop yourself.

This compulsion, this uncontrollable desire, drives the addict to take another drink, take another pill, place another bet, engage in whatever self-destructive behavior that they are controlled by. And that compulsion is just as strong as the uncontrollable need to breathe. For people who have been addicted, like me, it is very easy to understand what someone is feeling and fighting. But we aren't them. We understand in a general way that allows us to relate to them. To be able to communicate with them in a real way. But we aren't able to truly feel what they feel.

For people who have never been addicted, who have never felt that unreasonable and uncontrollable compulsion, it is almost impossible to understand, to relate to what the addict is feeling. Not being able to understand does not make anyone bad or wrong. But it leads to misunderstandings and frustration that often hurts the effort to overcome addiction, or to help someone who is trying to.

There is one thing that I believe, in my deepest heart, is the same for every addict. I have read many opinions from "experts" that don't share my opinion, but I still believe it to be true. And without believing, without accepting this truth, ending addiction might never be achieved. What is that truth?

Only the addict can fix themselves.

That is not to say that they won't need help, support, or a reason. It might be family. It might be a counselor or rehab facility. It could be a pastor. It could be a stranger. Wherever they find the tools that help them, they have to be the wielder of those tools. No one can do it for them. No matter how bad we want to help someone stop, make them, coerce, force, manipulate, or beg, it will fail if the addict doesn't want to stop. Everything will fail if the addict doesn't want to fix themselves, if they don't believe that they have a problem, and they still choose to use the substance or engage in the behavior.

Addicts will give countless excuses and reasons why they can't overcome their addiction. Past trauma, anxiety, failed relationships, not receiving a promotion, or whatever else you can think of. They will blame anything and everything, except themselves, for their failure to overcome their addiction. But they will be lying. They fail because they don't want to stop. They fail because they make the choice to do it again.

To overcome addiction, to win, requires something that is at once very profound and very simple. They have to want to stop. Them. The addict. Not the addict's mom. Or brother. Son. Daughter. Best friend. The addict has to come to the realization that they want to stop. They have to make a choice. The choice to stop letting the addiction win.

They have to want to overcome their addiction. They have to want to be sober, to stop the self-destruction, whatever it is. THE ADDICT has to want it. Until they do, they will continue to fail and continue to be under the control of their addiction. Maybe it sounds a little like I'm repeating myself. I am. Because anyone who wants someone to get sober, to overcome their addiction, has to understand that no matter how bad they want it for the addict, only when the addict wants it is there a chance for success.

The addict must have a desire, a motivation, a reason to stop the substance or behavior that they are addicted to. It has to come from within themselves. For me, seeing my daughter following my shameful example was what got my attention. That day in that courtroom, and the words that judge said to me, was my wakeup call. It was the moment that I finally saw in myself what everyone else had been seeing. And I didn't like it. That day, those two events sparked a desire to finally, however pitifully late it was, be the father that my daughters deserved. It gave me motivation to fix myself, something that only I could do. It was much more than that simple description, but that part of the story will wait a little longer.

Getting sober, stopping the drug use that I had done for too long, was the hardest thing I've ever done. Not only was it physically painful, but emotionally as well. I will tell you all about it as we continue this journey. But for now, I will just say that I doubted many times if I could do it. I questioned my resolve, my will, my strength. I didn't go through it alone. I had to start the process alone. I had to want to stop. I had to make another choice. The right choice.

Getting sober, overcoming addiction is not easy. It is painful. It is heartbreaking. It is spirit breaking. It can be a very long process. It can push you, the addict, and the ones that love them, to your breaking point. It can take you places you never, in your wildest dreams, imagined you would go. Physically, mentally, and emotionally. Sometimes, often, all at the same time.

Detoxing is part of the process. Cambridge Online Dictionary defines detoxification as "the process of removing harmful chemicals from something." It is the process of ridding the body of alcohol, drugs, or whatever chemical that is harming the person, that the person is addicted to. Medical detoxification can involve medications, supervision, and more provided by medical professionals and facilities that have experience, training, and resources to help the addicted person remove the toxic chemicals from their bodies safely. Detoxing can be very painful. If it is not managed properly by qualified professionals, detoxing can lead to short- or long-term health, emotional, and mental problems, and can be fatal. Detoxing affects people differently. It is NOT SAFE to attempt to detox without consulting medical professionals; physical, mental, and emotional. While you might be tempted to help an addict detox without proper, professional assistance, you could jeopardize their health, their mental and emotional future, and even their life. ALWAYS consult medical professionals and enlist their assistance.

Getting sober is not only the most difficult fight most addicts will ever face. It is potentially the most dangerous, too. For yourself, or for someone you care about and want to see overcome addiction, you owe it to everyone affected to do it right. Whatever that means, whatever that takes. There is no shame in asking for help.

Getting sober isn't as simple as "just stop." Getting sober isn't easy. But it is possible. To begin the journey that will, hopefully, bring the addict to sobriety, the addict just has to make the choice to take the first step.

Chapter 9: Living the life!

I have never met anyone who told me that they wanted to become an addict. I never shared a beer with anyone whose goal was to become an alcoholic. I never did drugs with anyone who wanted to lose themselves to a substance, destroy any positive relationships in their life, or everything they had ever had. No one starts doing anything to become addicted. It just happens. And when that demon gets a grip, the claws sink deep.

Every addict has a different story to tell. But every story has a shared starting point. Choice. We chose to do something – drink alcohol, take drugs, or whatever it is – that became a central focal point in our lives. It pushed out other things like family, responsibility, and rational thinking. Very few people take that first drink and are forever lost to the bottom of a bottle. Most don't take their first pill, smoke their first marijuana joint, hit the first crack pipe, and have no option but to continue. Making the choice to try a substance or activity the first time, however, often leads to repetition, and through continued use, addiction is the destination. By choosing to continue the behavior, whatever it is, we inadvertently make the choice to become an addict. And it is true that some substances are addictive with the first use. But the choice to do it the first time is still a choice.

Most of the time, the downward spiral starts slowly, with large, sweeping arcs and curves that don't allow us to see that we are starting a downward trend. It might seem harmless to stop at a bar after work and have a few drinks with friends. Maybe you like to have a beer while you cut the grass or do other outdoor activities. You go, with family or friends, to a ball game and have a couple of beers while you watch the game. Having friends over to watch a sporting event on TV is often accompanied by alcohol and snacks. None of which appears to have a negative or long-lasting effect on your life, your status quo. You enjoy your day, you enjoy the company, the drinking, and everything that goes with it. Then you return to your "normal life"; family, work, and responsibility. No one seems to suffer, no one is denied your attention or not receiving the things that they need or want. It all seems like harmless fun and, as we often see in movies, television shows, books, and social media, no one gets hurt. It is all just the way it is supposed to be.

It might start out as one or two, then home and a return to responsibilities, family, and life as it has been. Then it turns into three. Four. Then you don't make it home for dinner. You aren't there to help your children with their homework. Some of the bills are behind because you don't have the money to pay them. It can lead to arguments with your spouse, and other problems with family. You might stay out too late or get so drunk that you don't wake up on time and are late for work. Or miss work entirely.

The example above uses alcohol as the substance, but it can be anything. It could be that you share a joint with friends after work or on the weekends. It might be that you like to play the digital slot machine at the store you visit after work, or place a bet through an online app. It can be anything that starts to become more important than your responsibilities. We will just use alcohol, as it is one of the most common addictions, to keep it simple and allow us to focus on the life, not the substance or behavior.

That being said, it can also be a completely unintended process. As described earlier, people become sick or injured and begin taking medications to help them recover. The process, the situation, is the same. Only the starting point has changed. As I also told you before, the choice to take more than is prescribed, or to use medications for results they are not intended to produce, is dangerous and often leads to addiction. So, misusing medications is really no different than choosing to consume more and more alcohol, use drugs, and move on to stronger, more illicit drugs, or to engage in other harmful and self-destructive behaviors. As the purpose of this part of the story is not to define or explain addiction or the different things people become addicted to, we will not stray from what we are trying to understand.

The beginning is often a slow, drawn-out process and, therefore, isn't easily seen and stopped. We become accustomed to subtle changes. We allow things that we don't necessarily like but aren't "big enough" to fight about. We even justify many behavioral changes. Maybe he had a bad day at work. Maybe the electric bill was higher this month because it was unusually hot, and the air conditioning was used more than normal. We try to rationalize the changes in behavior and explain them without placing blame on the person who is changing. It is possible that we don't see that the choices they are making are causing the changes in their behavior. It could be that we don't realize that the one beer after work has increased to six, or more, and that the two or three on "game day" has become a full twelve pack. Because the increase was gradual, because it was done over a period of time, we didn't pay attention to the increase and now don't realize that it was the problem. Maybe it was because we didn't want to see it. We didn't want to start an argument over how many beers they were consuming each time. We didn't want to make them feel that they were being called out, criticized, or judged for what they were doing. It could be that we even accepted it and the increases we were seeing by making the "bad day," or other, excuses for them. Or that we were too caught up with our own priorities that we just weren't paying attention. Whatever the reason, however we got to that point, the beginning was slow and, often times, we didn't see it coming.

As the person falls further into addiction, things often become more noticeable. Financial struggles become more noticeable. One car payment might be missed, the cable bill didn't get paid, and was turned off, or some other deadline was missed. In the beginning, it can often be explained as a simple oversight, a minor mistake. Being late for work might be written off as beyond a person's control because of heavy traffic, a flat tire, or some other excuse. These little red flags might be few and far between in the early stages of addiction. And can be forgiven if they aren't repeated regularly, and the explanation is believable. And also, if we don't want to see the beginning of a pattern.

As the addiction progresses, so do the missteps. Being late for work every once in a while might turn into every week. Or every day. The car payments might fall behind by two or three. Maybe a weekend outing has to be cancelled because there isn't any money for it. Sometimes these things won't show themselves quickly but take weeks or months. But as the addict falls further into their behavior, it will start to gain momentum. The late and missed payments will come more regularly. The missed time at work will begin to draw negative attention. The excuses won't seem as valid.

Sometimes, an addict will see that they are having trouble obtaining the money needed to feed their addiction. If they have accumulated things — tools, multiple vehicles, memorabilia, or anything of value — they might start to sell or pawn their possessions to get the additional money that they need. If asked why they are selling things, they might make the excuse that they no longer need it, don't want it anymore, or aren't interested in it. They won't admit that they are selling the things to cover up the missing funds that they need to keep up the fiction of their life. When they run out of things that belong to them, other things could turn up missing. Jewelry, electronics, or other things that belong to others – family or friends – could be "lost" or "mis-placed" in an attempt to keep the cover-up going.

Many times, the addict will be unable to see that the substance and their behavior is the direct cause of all of their problems. They will not understand that the choices that they have made have brought them to this point. They will fail to understand why their excuses aren't working any longer and will likely resent being questioned about the circumstances or their behaviors.

Eventually, it becomes impossible to hide. Anything that could be sold is gone, any other means of obtaining money has been exhausted. Many times, when reaching this point, the addict will reach out to other family or friends to borrow money. They will make excuses that can seem legitimate and often seem reasonable. Many times, people will be willing to help, to loan them the money that they need to meet an obligation. "Work was slow this month, and I'm struggling to pay the rent." "My car broke down and, after paying to get it fixed, I'm not able to make my payment." Or any other excuse that they can think of. And for people who either aren't aware of the addict's substance abuse, or don't want to see it, it can be easier to "help" than to question them.

But at some point, all of the excuses, all of the pleading, all options, are exhausted. When the problem reaches the point that it can no longer be ignored, many things are possible. A marriage could end. The addict's spouse could simply decide, or realize, that they can't take anymore and make the choice to end the marriage to escape the destruction. Friends can turn away. Missing too much time at work will likely lead to termination and a complete loss of income.

When their backs are against the wall, many addicts will become angry and lash out at others. I have been told stories by many people that when their child asked for more money, and they were told no, that they became enraged. They often threatened, or committed, violence. They would yell and verbally or physically attack the person who would not, or could not, give them any more assistance. They would often see themselves as victims, unfairly denied what they wanted simply because the other person didn't want to give it to them. Many addicts would accuse the other person of doing something wrong – accusing a spouse of cheating, a parent of not loving them, a friend of being jealous and trying to hold them down – in an attempt to cause them harm, pain, and misery. They might steal from family, friends, or businesses in an attempt to get access to money to feed their addiction. I have heard people tell family and friends that we won't "help" them because we want to see them homeless.

There are many documented stories of elderly parents locking themselves in their bedrooms to escape the onslaught of an addicted child going into a rage because they weren't given what they wanted. Addiction isn't limited to the young. It can affect anyone, anywhere, any age. Situations where an adult child is addicted to a substance, has lost everything, and begged and been allowed to move back into their parent's home. They are usually, by this time, deeply lost in their addiction and are toxic in their childhood home. They usually won't work, refuse to do anything to help around the house, and feel that they are entitled. Entitled to financial help, or handouts, to be allowed to do as they please, and since they are adults, they should not have to answer for anything that they say or do. They can exploit their parents' love and attempts to help to the extent that their parents become depressed, financially unstable, and their health can become negatively affected. As the tension grows between the addict and the family, the situation described above can become reality. An addict asks for something – money, to use the parents' car, or pretty much anything – and is denied. The parents might not have the money to give, can't risk someone under the influence driving their vehicle and placing them at risk, or say no to any request or demand. The addict becomes frustrated and angry. They begin lashing out at the parents for not giving in. It often starts with verbal assaults, insults, and accusations. The addict will try to intimidate their parents to get whatever they want. If this doesn't work, the situation can escalate to threats of physical violence, or to actual physical violence. Addicts under the influence or who are feeling the cravings and compulsions of addiction are unpredictable and often do not stop to think, or realize, that they are threatening and hurting the people that they love. They are so lost in their addiction that the only thing that matters to them is getting their way or getting their next "fix." While it sounds outrageous, there are too many documented cases of parents, or others, having to barricade themselves in their homes, or in rooms in their homes, to escape the violence of an addict who won't take no for an answer. Many are hesitant, or afraid, to call for help. They don't want to see someone that they love arrested for being under the influence, in possession of an illegal substance, or for the violence that they are threatening or have committed. Many times, they will give in to the addict in an attempt to calm them, to get them to stop the threats, insults, and attacks. They will give in even though they know they shouldn't. Out of love, of fear, or because they are overwhelmed and don't know what else to do.

Parents are often the target of the addicts pleading and the unpleasant actions that can follow. But they are not the only potential targets for the addict. Many spouses have experienced varied forms of abuse from addicts. The same insults, threats, accusations, and abuse that is directed at parents are often directed at the person's spouse first. Accusations of infidelity, of hiding money or other items, of not loving them, and countless others are also part of the onslaught that a spouse can have to face. I have even heard of cases where the addict accuses their spouse of being responsible for their addiction, their substance abuse, their self-destructive behavior. Many, when confronted by other family members or friends, throw their spouse under the bus by saying that their spouse provides the substance and encourages the addict to consume it. I have been told stories of a spouse being accused of hiding the addict's drugs, of destroying them. Or that jewelry, including wedding rings, has mysteriously disappeared, and the addict becomes indignant or defensive if questioned. And, sadly, these verbal assaults too often escalate to physical violence. Many spouses are physically and emotionally abused because they do not support the addict's behavior, drug use, or the new person they have become. Some spouses try to hide this abuse, lie for the addict, or make excuses in an attempt to hide their problem, and refuse to hold the addict accountable for their actions. The situation usually escalates until the spouse can't take it anymore and leaves. Or worse.

Children are also often the targets and victims of the addict's outbursts. From young children to grown, adult children, the reality is that an addict will target anyone they see as someone they can manipulate to give in to them. They can also belittle or neglect their children. In addition to all of the things that they do to and accuse their parents or spouses of. And, as with parents and spouses, the abuse can escalate and become physical.

No one is safe from the addict. Addicts can prey on, attempt to threaten or manipulate, or intimidate anyone in their lives. Family is usually the most common target, but friends, co-workers, employers, and even strangers can become the target of an addict who is focused on getting what they need to feed and continue their addiction.

There are stories of people who weren't able to escape the attack and were killed because an addict cared more about getting what they wanted than who they were attacking. While most stories don't end with those results, enough do. One is enough. One is too many. Never underestimate the potential for an addict to act in irrational or possibly violent ways to get what they want. Whether they would do those things or act that way if they weren't under the influence of their addiction does not matter. What matters is your protection, your safety. Your sanity. Your life.

If you or a loved one is in a situation like this, where you or they are being threatened, attacked, or abused, or treated in any way that makes you feel unsafe, contact local authorities for protection and assistance. Do not ever allow yourself to be intimidated, verbally or physically assaulted, or mistreated in any way because you won't give in to an out-of-control addict. Do not worry about hurting

74

their feelings, or if they will get in trouble and go to jail. Make your safety your priority and sort everything else out later. NEVER be afraid to call for help if you feel unsafe or threatened. They might be upset because you seek help and protection. They might say hurtful things. But all that matters is, again, your safety, your sanity, and your life.

Chapter 10: The manipulation game

As an addict falls deeper under the spell of their personal demon, the addiction takes more of their time, their focus, and other things start to slip through the cracks. Bills don't get paid because the money went to satisfy the need for whatever substance has taken hold. When others – family, friends, a spouse – start to notice, the addict often starts to weave a web of lies to escape. The addict will come up with any reason they can to redirect the questions, the accusations, and the reality that they have created.

An addict will often turn to manipulation. Manipulation can come in many forms and is often subtle. From trying to make others feel sorry for them, have pity for their situation, to trying to convince someone they aren't seeing what their eyes are showing them, manipulation is a way that an addict will attempt to escape responsibility. When an addict feels that they are being cornered, they will usually try to escape by running, denying, and trying to make the situation go away. An addict will invent stories and scenarios that seek to explain the real situation by weaving a story that makes them the victim instead of the guilty one. It's never their fault, someone was out to get them, they have really bad luck, or some other reason to remove responsibility from them and place it somewhere, anywhere, else.

Many times, the addict is allowed to get away with their manipulations because we don't want to hurt their feelings. We know that they are lying to us, but we don't call them out because we don't want to make the situation worse. We rationalize that by not escalating the problem, that somehow, we can achieve a good outcome because we don't let the situation turn into an altercation. By responding to the manipulation in this way, we train the addict that their lies and evasion are working, that they have fooled us, and that we believe their made-up stories. This often leads to bigger lies and rarely, if ever, actually helps the addict.

When an addict thinks that their gaslighting and manipulation is working, they will gain confidence that they are hiding their addiction, and the associated problems, from others. This can lead to more problems because they think that everyone is blaming something else for their actions and problems, so they push further into the bad behaviors. Instead of admitting that they have a problem, and that their choices are the cause of their situation, they invent more stories and dig the hole deeper, trying to escape blame. Eventually, the house of cards that they build starts to fall. When the collapse begins, it is impossible to stop and can lead to the addict lashing out, verbally or physically, at others that are only trying to help them. By letting the lies grow, the stories become too far-fetched, the result, when the truth is finally revealed, is often very unpleasant.

Sometimes, when the addict's behavior becomes noticeable to others, they will try to make you believe you aren't seeing what you think you are seeing. They will try to deflect questions, change the conversation, or end the conversation to avoid having to answer uncomfortable questions. There are many ways an addict will try to convince you that you don't understand what is happening, that your perspective is wrong, and that you are incorrect in your accusations.

An addict will do whatever they can to escape anything that will show that they are at fault. For example, if an addict loses a job, they will often blame anything but themselves and their actions for the loss or inability to find another job. They might use any excuse they can think of for having lost their job in the first place. The story could be that the company is having to cut back, downsize, and that they are an unfortunate and innocent victim of circumstance. They won't admit that because of the substance use, they were late many times. Or absent without an excusable reason, or beyond the limit of what is allowed. They will never tell you that their job performance had slipped, and their work had suffered because of the substance abuse. It would always be that something, or someone, had caused the situation that led to their termination.

The story might be that someone at work was jealous of their work and had begun spreading lies about them or sabotaging their work, creating a situation that led to the loss of their job. Depending on the position that they held, it could sound reasonable and potentially believable. And sometimes, because we don't want to believe that someone we care about would be self-destructive and responsible for what happened, we accept the story without too many questions.

Another way that addicts use manipulation is to attack those that question them. Continuing the example above, if the addict is questioned about the details of the story, they could try to turn the argument around. They could accuse the one asking questions of not believing them, blaming them, or of not listening to what they are being told. Addicts often use anger as a way to deflect questions that they don't want to, or can't, answer. They will attack their spouse, their parents, friends, or anyone else, because to be honest would place the blame and guilt on them.

Addicts use manipulation to try to get what they want and make their lives easier. They manipulate people and situations to shift blame and responsibility to anything or anyone other than themselves. They portray themselves as victims to get sympathy and get what they want.

I know of people who have suffered addiction for many years and have used their own addiction as a manipulation tool. They will finally go to a family member or friend and tell them that they have a problem and want help. They are usually accomplished actors by this point and can come off as very convincing. This point usually comes after all their other plans and manipulations have failed, and they are left with very few choices. And it is often easy to allow ourselves to believe that the addict has really turned a corner because we want that for them so badly.

For example, imagine that you have a family member who is an alcoholic. After years of excuses, years of failed plans to get their lives together, you have finally reached a point where you call them out on their lies and failures. But this time, instead of blowing up, getting mad, and running off, they tell you that, yes, they have a problem and really want to get help. The reversal of direction can often fool us into thinking that they have finally seen the light and are ready to get sober. It might be the truth. But most of the time, it isn't. It is just another attempt to manipulate you into seeing them as a victim, having pity for them, and opening yourself to try to help them. Since you have shown them that you don't believe the lies and excuses, blaming others for all of their mistakes, they are trying a different tactic. They think that you will let your guard down if they appear vulnerable and that sympathy will help them get what they want. And that you will stop being critical of them and their actions and behaviors, and be more willing to believe them. Some addicts will carry this manipulation to extremes and do things that appear to be sincere, real attempts to get sober, while they are just buying time and working on a plan to get what they want.

Many addicts will tell you that they want to go to rehab to get help. They think that by telling you that they want rehab, not that they are being made to go, that you will believe that they are serious about getting sober. Again, maybe. And, sadly, maybe not. When an addict has used up all the sympathy and goodwill that family and friends have offered, when they have nowhere else to turn and are facing homelessness, they can see rehab as a place to go to have a roof over their head. They can see it as a place where they will be fed, protected, and kept off the streets. If that is all that they are seeking, they will never say that out loud. They will think that they have convinced you that they are serious about getting sober, manipulate you into supporting them. They might make you believe that while they are serious and want to be sober, they can't afford the rehab or any other costs or necessities that they need while they are going through the process. They will tell a story of how hard it will be, how impossible, to complete the rehab process if they can't work, can't earn a living, and how if they had assistance that they would be successful.

Some enter rehab because they have no choice. Many are given the option of spending time in jail or spending time in a rehab facility. Given those choices, most choose rehab. They enter the program with no intention of getting sober. They do it only to satisfy the requirements imposed by the court. Family can also give an addict the ultimatum of rehab or nothing, and the addict will go to appease the family. These addicts are wasting the time and resources of the rehab facility and taking away an opportunity for someone who really wants help. But they will sing the praises of rehab, shout to anyone who will listen how they are going to get sober and get their lives on track. All the while knowing that every word they say is a lie meant to manipulate the system, their families, and the rehab facility.

If an addict enters a rehab facility without a genuine desire to find help and sobriety, failure is the only eventual outcome. They might complete the program, "graduate", get their sobriety chips and certificates. They might use those to further manipulate people that care for them into believing that they have achieved sobriety. When in reality they are only using their "success" as a way to get someone to give them more help, more money, to believe their lies, so that they can continue to indulge in their addiction without recrimination. They might attend meetings after they leave the rehab to show those watching that they are "serious" about staying sober.

They are hoping that the people watching, the people that care about them, will believe that they are doing better and that they are on the right path. They will want them to let their guards down so that they won't see when things start reverting to what led to the problems in the beginning. And, if allowed, they will start the whole process over. Often leading to a repeat of everything that has already happened. Life destroyed, others hurt and used, and back to the "I need help" story. And because we care about them, we want to see them get sober, we often allow this pattern to continue and repeat over and over again. Because the addict has said that without help, they will end up living on the streets, or worse. Because we don't want to see that happen to someone we care about, we often continue to allow the cycle to continue, uninterrupted and unbroken.

Many times, the story the addict has told us, that a life of despair and homelessness, with nothing and no one, is all that they have to look forward to is the only truth the addict has told us. They will hold that truth up and tell you that you don't care. That you want to see them living on the streets. That you don't want them to have anything or have people in their lives. They will tell you that it will be your fault if they end up this way and try to use that guilt to get you to provide shelter, money, or whatever it is that they want. While that bleak future is true for many addicts, using it to get sympathy and "help" is just manipulation. While that sad and pitiful future is a real possibility for them, they want you to be, to feel, responsible for it. They do not want to be told that their actions, their choices, are the reason that that destination is their future. They are unwilling to do what is necessary to ensure that that future doesn't happen and want someone else to fix it and provide an escape. They use guilt as a manipulation tool to achieve that end.

Many addicts that enter rehab will tell family or friends that the conditions are horrible, that they are mistreated, and are not receiving the help that was promised. And, sadly, sometimes it is true. But many times, it is really that the addict is rejecting the help that is offered, doesn't want to be in rehab, and is only trying to manipulate people into believing that they shouldn't be there. They are trying to get out of the rehab that they said they wanted, they are trying to escape forced sobriety and are hoping that someone will pity them and tell them that they can leave, that they shouldn't waste their time if it isn't going to help. The addict will blame the facility, the system, the people that are trying to help them for the pending failure. They will not admit that they don't want help and are rejecting all attempts to provide help. They will tell a story, again, that makes them the victim and try to gain sympathy to escape blame and responsibility. Many will use this as an attempt to get family or friends to open their homes to them. And use that to extract everything that they can out of the situation: shelter, money, transportation, or whatever they can gain.

Another common use of manipulation is for the addict to tell someone that they admit that they have a problem, that they have a plan to get help, and that they need "just one more chance" to get it right. They will say that if you help them just one more time that they will be able to get out of the situation that has them held down and be on their way to a successful, sober future. They might say that, yes, they spent the money that was supposed to be for their rent on alcohol, but they realize their mistake, and if you'll just help them out, this one last time, they won't let it happen again. That they will get sober and not waste their money on alcohol. And because you want to believe them, to see them sober, and because they seem so sincere, you allow yourself to be manipulated by giving them the money, or other help that they are asking for. They probably have no intention of changing their behavior. They just want to have whatever they are addicted to and still be able to have money to pay their bills. The "one more time" story will often be used as many times as the addict can get you to fall for it. And it will never end, unless you refuse to play along, because there will ALWAYS be "just one more time."

I have also been told that the results of someone's addiction, the use of drugs and alcohol, the consequences of their choices and actions, are the REASON that they are continuing to feed their addiction. That they continue their behavior because of what they caused to happen. Let's say that a person has a child. And that person is, or becomes, an addict. There can be many paths that can diverge from this point.

One path goes something like this. A parent is raising their kids, working, providing a stable home, and, at some point, is exposed to a substance and makes the choice to use it. It could be drugs, alcohol. It could be anything. It could be that the parent was injured in an accident and prescribed medication, opiate pain pills for example, that they ultimately begin abusing and become addicted to. It could be that they are in a situation where they have a choice to try a drug, consume alcohol, or whatever it is that they become addicted to, and make the choice to do it without a reason. As their life continues, they might be able to keep it together for a while, for years even. But then it all starts to unravel. The addiction begins to creep further into their every day, and the stability starts to falter. The kids might have grown up some, might be teenagers by the time that everything starts to fall apart. They might start to pull away from the addicted parent, to not like what they see in them, and reject that addictive behavior. But the parent is too caught up in their addiction to understand that it is because of their addiction that their children are pulling away. So, they make the excuse that because their children have rejected them, because they don't have a good relationship with their kids, that they are depressed and need the substance to help them cope. So, they take the drugs, drink the alcohol, or whatever it is, to numb the pain. It doesn't only apply to drugs and alcohol. It can apply to any addiction.

Some people have gambling addictions. They spend time away from their families, going to casinos or secluding themselves in a room, gambling online, taking themselves away from their families. When the family is pushed to the point that they just turn away, the gambler might say that everyone has abandoned them and that they participate in the card games to not be alone. They refuse to see, or refuse to acknowledge, that their behavior caused them to lose their family and instead use the loss as justification to continue their behavior.

A person who claims to have a sex addiction might lose their family because of infidelity. If they engage in their behavior, leaving their families – spouses, children – and ultimately lose that family because of it, they could say that they continue because they don't want to be alone. Even after the family is broken by divorce, the addicted person could continue to push their children or other extended family away by choosing random partners over their family. Again, refusing to admit that their addition, their choices, their behavior caused the problem.

They could end up in a situation where their children are taken from them by the court system or other family members. They could lose custody of their children, have limited or restricted visitation, or lose them entirely. And then make the excuse that because they feel so guilty, or so mistreated by the system, that they can't deal with their lives and use drugs, consume alcohol, or whatever it is, to help them continue to get by. And again, refuse to see that their addiction, their decisions, their actions caused the outcome that they use as the excuse to continue their self-destruction.

I have been told that a man's wife left him because he wouldn't stop drinking. And that he drinks now because he's sad that she's gone. When all he had to do to keep her from leaving was to stop drinking. If he'd just stopped drinking, she would still be with him, and he wouldn't be sad that she was gone. But he was selfish and refused, told her he wasn't hurting her, abusing her, mistreating her. That she was being controlling by telling him she'd leave him. He blamed her, told her, and everyone else that she was trying to hold him back, not let him be himself. And while he didn't physically abuse her, did work and pay his bills, he was still hurting her. Seeing him drunk every night, every day he wasn't at work, caused her emotional pain. In reality, he spent his time with alcohol, not her. She was denied the relationship that they had originally built and was, essentially, left to live her life alone watching him spend his time with alcohol. But he refused to see it. When she kept her word and left, he continued to drink and blamed her. He said his alcohol abuse was all because she had left him, because he was hurt and sad. Refused to remember that his alcohol abuse had left her alone in their marriage and, in the end, caused her to leave.

I have also known people that would trade one substance or behavior for another. An alcoholic might be able to stop drinking but fall victim to another addiction. I have seen people get sober from alcohol but become addicted to opiate pain pills. Transferring the addiction doesn't solve the problem. But they got mad when it was pointed out and said that they had quit drinking, and that alcohol had always been the problem. That they didn't have a problem anymore. But they did. It was just another substance. Their behaviors, their choices, and their actions were the same.

All of those examples are manipulation. Manipulation isn't just about people. It's about facts, details, the stories that the addict tells to justify their behaviors, themselves, and to keep blame from being focused on them.

Manipulation is typically the preferred tool of an addict. Some are willing to use threats and physical violence, but most try to avoid that as it will probably lead to law enforcement involvement and jail. Some use coercion, another form of manipulation, to get what they want. Some try to bribe or beg. But in the end, any of these methods are manipulation. Anything that the addict does to get you to give them what they want, to allow them to escape responsibility and consequences, is allowing them to manipulate you. It is not their desire to get help or to get sober, it is their desire to continue their addiction, their self-destructive behaviors, without accountability or recrimination that is the ultimate goal. It is their tool to get the means to the end that they desire.

Allowing an addict to manipulate you is not helping the addict. It is only extending the inevitable. It doesn't help their health, as they are allowed to continue to abuse whatever substance they are addicted to. It doesn't help their mental state, as it teaches them that it is acceptable to use people, to take advantage of people, only to gain their selfish desires and ends. It doesn't teach them responsibility because they are allowed to escape the consequences of their choices and actions.

Not all manipulators are addicts. But all addicts are, or will try to be, manipulators. Addicts don't like to be called out, don't like to be shown that they are the problem. Addicts will push manipulation as far as they can, and as far as they are allowed. They will try everything imaginable to get the heat off of them and be able to continue their addiction and behavior. It doesn't mean that they are bad people. It is another example of how they are affected by their addiction and shows how far they will go to continue their behavior.

Addicts can become violent. If the manipulation isn't getting them what they want, they can lash out. I have, as mentioned earlier, heard stories of people attacking family members because they refused to give them money for drugs or alcohol. I have heard stories where addicts refused to leave their parents' or friends' homes, saying that they had nowhere else to go and that they only wanted to see them homeless. Addicts have stolen money and other things from family and friends, stolen from stores, and done whatever they had to do to get their substance.

Allowing yourself to be manipulated is not healthy either. Giving in to an addict, to their manipulations and desires, can cause many problems for the person who only cares and wants to help the addict. I know of many cases of lives that have been devastated, ruined because people were unknowingly, or willingly, manipulated. I have seen people financially ruined, bankrupted, trying to help an addict. I have seen people suffer health problems because they are so worried and stressed because of the addict's behavior. Stress and anxiety cause many health problems without the added layer of dealing with an addict. It is difficult to deny someone we care about something that they want. But when dealing with an addict, sometimes we have to. If we allow the manipulation to continue, to succeed, we are only harming ourselves and the addicted person that we love.

Many addicts refuse to seek help. They will tell you that they have everything under control, that they have a plan, that they've "got this." They won't seek counseling because they feel like they would be looked down on, seen as weak, or some other excuse. When the reality is that they don't want to face their demons and addiction. They don't want to have their failures laid out and have to look at them. They will make every excuse to avoid getting help, talking to someone, and facing the truth. They will manipulate themselves, allow their addiction to cloud their judgement, and make them think that they can make it to sobriety alone.

And when an addict has manipulated everyone – friends, family, the legal system, everyone – for so long that nobody believes them anymore, it can create more problems if or when the addict really does want to get sober. Because of the years of lies, the games that have been played, and the hurt that has been caused, it can be difficult for the addict to convince anyone that they are serious about getting help. It can be hard to believe them because of all the times you've tried before. All the times you've given them the benefit of the doubt. All because the addict used every trick and manipulation they could for so long to twist reality and allow them to continue to live that life.

If an addict does want to get sober, does want to beat their addiction, they most likely won't be able to do it alone. If they have spent years manipulating everyone, how are they supposed to prove that this time is real? The same way they proved that they were an addict. Choice and action. They have to make the choice to get sober. The addict has to make the choice. It cannot be made for them by anyone else. Ever, ever, ever, ever, period. And action. They have to take the first step toward getting sober. Alone. No one can take that step for them. They have to commit themselves to whatever it takes to get sober. Very few people can beat addiction alone. They have to find a reputable, real rehab or counselor and start the process. Without fanfare, without self-congratulation, and without anyone forcing them. They have to accept that it is a hard battle and a long journey. And they have to start it alone. Because in most cases, they have already made everyone who wanted it for them and cared about them doubt that it would never happen. They have to show everyone that they are serious and will not fail again. Words won't do it. Only the action of actually getting sober. And staying sober.

It will take time to regain trust that is lost to an addict's manipulation. But the addict has to accept this and be willing to do whatever is necessary to regain that lost trust. It might not ever be possible. And if it's not, then the addict has to accept that. Without recrimination toward anyone who has lingering doubts. If an addict can get sober and stay sober, the trust will come back. It, like getting sober in the first place, takes time and can't be rushed or forced. That is just the cost of using manipulation.

Chapter 11: Helping isn't really helping...

Addicts often ask for help. Money for rent, groceries, gas, other bills. A place to live while they get through tough times. Anything that they want or need that they don't have a way to obtain, they will try to get from someone else. They will come up with reasons that they need help, like we talked about in the Manipulation Game, and will often be relentless until the "help" is given to them. But is giving in and "helping" really helping them? Or is it allowing them to continue their addiction, their self-destructive behavior, and continue on the path to the disaster and the end of that road?

Helping an addict is more often ENABLING than really helping. Merriam Webster's online dictionary gives the following definition of enabling: 1a: to provide with the means or opportunity; b: to make possible, practical, or easy; c: to cause to operate. The parts of this definition that apply most accurately to an addict are a and b. Because without "help," the addict would often be unable to meet their real-world responsibilities and still be able to feed their addiction.

Enabling is most often done with good intentions. As I have said many times already, we don't want to see someone we care about suffer. So, we try to find ways to minimize that suffering. Especially when the story that we're being told sounds plausible.

Addicts will, as I said, use manipulation to get what they want. They might come to you and say I can't pay my rent, and I'm going to end up on the streets and lose everything I have. If you give in and pay that rent, you are only giving them a place to continue to live out their addiction. It often starts small. The addict will tell you they are a little short on their electric bill, insurance, or something else and ask if you can let them "borrow" a little money to pay it.

And they will continue to "borrow" as long as they are allowed to.

When you give an addict money for anything, you are really purchasing the substance that they are addicted to. If they still have their drugs, but can't pay the car insurance, they spent the insurance money on drugs. When you give them the money to make the payment, you are replacing the money that they spent on drugs. Hence, you are buying the drugs for them.

I have had many people argue with me that they are not buying the drugs, the alcohol, the whatever. But they are. If the addict had the money to buy the substance, then they had the money to pay the bill. Had they not purchased the beer, the dope, or whatever it is, that money would have been available to put toward their financial obligations. But they chose to spend it on their addiction and ask you to make up the difference. Replacing the money, even if it then goes toward the bill, is still buying the substance for the addict. Trying to justify giving an addict money by saying it is for a specific purpose is denying the truth. That the money replacing what they had and spent on their addiction is really providing the money to buy it in the first place.

Another form of enabling is allowing the addict to continue their behavior. We don't want the addict to be mad at us, so we often don't say anything. Our silence is our consent. Our consent enables the addict and, in their mind, is our approval. Since we didn't tell them not to do it, didn't try to talk them out of it, we must be accepting and approving of the continued behavior. This can lead to bigger problems and arguments later when we do try to stop them from doing whatever it is that they are addicted to. They might say that we haven't said anything before, so they thought that we accepted what they were doing. They might try to turn it around and say that we are only trying to stop them now because we want something from them, or that we are trying to control them, which is a manipulation to get us to stop.

Most addicts are enabled by those that care about them in the beginning. It is normal to not want to believe that someone we care about is drinking too much, using drugs, or engaging in some other self-destructive behavior. So, we choose not to "see" it in the beginning. Maybe we hope that it will stop, just be a phase, and that the addict will "see the light" and change their ways on their own. Maybe we don't like confrontation and fear what the result of confronting them would be. Maybe we are so busy with our own lives and responsibilities that we really don't notice the early signs. We don't see it until it's too late.

Enabling an addict is not only destructive to the addict, but it can also damage us too. If we give in to their financial needs, we might not be able to meet our obligations and fall behind ourselves. I have been told that I wanted to see someone homeless. Because I refused to continue handing over money week after week to pay for their addiction. They didn't see it as paying for their addiction, they saw it as me "helping" pay their bills. I was expected to pay for their lives, essentially, and allow them to spend what money they did have on a self-destructive substance. And I wasn't supposed to complain. When I did, it turned ugly. I was told that I wanted to see them homeless, wanted them to lose all of their belongings, and that I didn't care about them.

Part of the escalation, the accusations, was my fault. It was my fault because I had given in too many times and had led them to believe that it would continue. Because I had not refused to provide the "help" for a long time, it was a shock when I finally said no more. And their response was anger. They lashed out at me and blamed me for the situation they were in. My answer was simple. That I had been wrong to ever provide the means for them to continue to purchase their preferred substance. And that I had to ensure that my wife and I wouldn't end up homeless because we couldn't pay our bills. I was more or less called a liar and told that I was just being stingy, that I was selfish because I wanted to spend the money on things I wanted.

That situation has happened with more than one person. That's why I generalized it. Different people responded in different ways. One I didn't speak to for over a year. One kept trying to find ways to manipulate my wife and me. One I haven't spoken to in several years. All are family. And it hurts.

It hurts to have to tell someone you love that you won't give them what they want. To deny them "help" because it really isn't help. Knowing that it's only allowing them to continue to harm themselves, knowing that it is only buying their alcohol or drugs, doesn't stop it from hurting when we see them suffer. We see them lose their possessions, lose their homes, have to move from friend to friend, to cheap run-down motels, even the street. Watching that causes pain that is very real and makes us want to give in, to provide whatever is necessary. To save them.

But enabling is never saving them. It is only putting off the inevitable. Making it possible for them to continue their path of self-destruction will only lead to more pain, more heartache, and more disappointment. And the outcome isn't always a happy one.

I had a coworker that had gotten clean from heroin. Through conversations with me and another coworker, he learned that we had both had addiction problems and been drug users. And that, like him, we had stopped using drugs years earlier. He felt comfortable talking to us, and we had many discussions about our past lives and the lessons we had learned. Time went on, and we all ended up working different shifts, so we didn't get to talk as much as we had. The coworker that had stopped using heroin started missing work. We asked him if he was ok, and he said that he had reconnected with an ex-girlfriend that he had a child with and had been taking time off to reconnect with his child. He wasn't missing work every day, he wasn't acting differently when we did get to talk to him. So, we didn't worry too much about it. We should have.

We should have asked more questions. We should have taken everything he had told us into consideration and realized that the ex-girlfriend was not only the mother of his child, but was someone he had a history of heroin use with. He had told us that he had used drugs with numerous ex-friends and ex-girlfriends. He had never told us specifically that he had used drugs with this particular girl. We didn't ask. Again, we should have.

A short time after his behavior changed, two or three weeks, he missed work. He didn't call in sick. He didn't come back. Most people assumed that he had just found another job and moved on. That was pretty common in the industry.

About two weeks after he stopped returning to work, one of the supervisors received a phone call. It was to let us know that he hadn't just quit. He had overdosed. It hit us hard, especially those of us who had shared many of our past secrets and shared his. We found out that he had indeed reconnected with his child, and also with his ex-girlfriend. She hadn't stopped using. She wanted him to join her again. He had refused for a while, but eventually gave in. He had been clean for a few years and died the first time he used with her again.

Maybe if we had asked more questions, we could have prevented it. Maybe he would have turned to us instead of giving in to her. But we didn't ask. And we will never know. We felt that we had enabled him by not asking those questions, by not seeing the danger that he could be facing. By letting him hide it from us. By not seeing.

Sometimes the outcome is tragic even if we do see. Even if we do question. Even if we do stop enabling and force the addict to go to rehab. It is very difficult to maneuver through life with an addict. The constant manipulation, the relentless asking for "help." It is a burden that no one should have to bear. It causes anxiety, arguments, anger, hurt feelings. And the only end is when the addict finally understands and does whatever it takes to fix themselves. Or when we lose them.

Fear of losing someone we love is not a reason to give in. It does not make it acceptable to enable an addict. It is a difficult path, but it must be taken. The best way is to never enable an addict. But that is, in my experience as an addict and a parent, quite difficult if not impossible. But it can't go on forever. Allowing it to destroy your life, the rest of their friends and family, is not the right course. As soon as you realize that you are enabling someone, you have to stop. Don't be cruel. Don't do it as a punishment. Just explain that you can't condone the continued behavior and that you won't be responsible for it any longer.

Never stop supporting them emotionally. Just don't do it financially, and don't condone their negative behaviors. Encourage them to seek real help.

Rehab, counseling, anything that will help them get control of themselves and their lives and leave the substance use behind them. When they do make a sincere attempt, be there for them. But be very vigilant and make sure that you aren't allowing the manipulation cycle to start over again. Don't enable them to fail. Hold them to their new commitment and watch them closely and often to make sure they don't stray from their new path.

Don't pretend to believe them. Be honest. If you don't believe that what you are being told is sincere or true, ask for proof. Addicts manipulate. Pretending to believe them is also enabling. Don't play that game. Ask them to prove that what they are telling you is true. They owe you that anyway. Don't be unreasonable with your demands, but don't be too soft either. Don't allow yourself to see something that isn't true. Look with your eyes wide open and don't let your eyes lie to you. If they are still engaging in their behavior, call them out. If they aren't, acknowledge it. Don't stop being watchful, but don't automatically distrust either. If they fail, which happens often as few get sober on the first or second real attempt, don't turn your back on them. Simply return to the position you have been holding, refuse to enable them. Refuse to be manipulated and help them find the strength to try again.

If you insist on enabling an addict, then enable them to succeed when they finally start to get it right. And hold them to it.

Chapter 12: Rehab

Something that most addicts face at some point on their journey to recovery is rehab. I will, in the spirit of full transparency, tell you that I have never been through a rehab program. I got clean with the help of some very good friends and family. I will tell you more about how I got clean later, but this needs to be addressed, so we're going to do it here and now. Having never been through a rehab program, I am not going to try to sell you on the wonderful benefits of rehab. I'm not going to tell you that they are useless and a waste of time. I'm going to give you my opinion based on research that I have done, people I've known that have been through rehab, and examples of some of the facilities that I have known of and been told about over many years. And, like everything else in this rambling dissertation, take from it what you will.

I have seen the ads on television that claim to work miracles. I have heard people say, "I used to be an addict." I've read and heard promises that make getting clean and sober sound easy, like a walk in the park. My experience, and the experiences of everyone I know that have been through this, tell a much different story. Getting clean is not easy. And it doesn't happen overnight. It takes time and commitment. And most of the time it takes help. A lot of help.

I have known people who didn't want to go to a rehab facility because of the stigma that they thought was attached. They felt that people would look down on them, think they were weak, and used many other excuses not to go into rehab. I believe that anyone making excuses is afraid. Afraid of failing. Afraid of letting people down. Maybe afraid of what others might say. But afraid of something. And many people let that fear stop them from taking the first step that would put them on the path to sobriety.

I have also known people that made excuses because they didn't want to stop. They didn't want to get clean, so they invented reasons to avoid getting help.

I have seen successes and failures. I have known people who had to go into rehab more than once, some a few times, before they found the combination of attitude and help that allowed them a real chance to get clean. Rehabs are all going to be different. And some won't be the answer for some addicts. Like every relationship in our lives, the chemistry has to be right. Personalities, life experience, and many other factors come into play. And for an addict that is already facing the immense challenges of stopping substance abuse, alcohol abuse, or whatever their demon is, the challenges are amplified. Getting clean and sober is difficult in many ways. It is physically challenging for most because our bodies have developed a dependence on a substance. Detox is very real and can be very painful. I have read of situations where people died during the detox process. As I told you earlier, consult a medical professional before attempting to detox. I am not trying to exaggerate the danger. I am not trying to scare anyone. I am telling you that you probably can't do it alone, and to do it the safest, most effective way, you will need a medical professional. Or a few.

Before you enter a program, do your homework. Look them up online, read everything you can about the program, the facility, the staff. Read reviews of people who have been through the program. You will undoubtedly find positive and negative reviews. Don't read just one. Read all you can find. And keep in mind that not everything works for every individual. What worked for one person might fail miserably for someone else. And what was a complete waste of time for one might be another's ticket to success. We are all different, and we must all direct our approach to what offers us the best chance of success. Getting clean, living sober is the goal. How we get there isn't the most important part. Getting there and staying there is.

As a family member, when the addict enters the rehab program, you must not interfere. You must allow the process to work. Many programs isolate the addict for a period of time. This is necessary to allow the addict time to detox, if necessary, and to get used to being in the program. Don't call constantly and demand to speak to the addict. Don't pester the staff with constant questions about their status. Allow them to do their job and help the addict. Before they enter the program, encourage them to work with the program, the staff, and do everything they can to help get them to a sober life. Let them know that you will be there when they need you and when they complete the program. But don't get in the way. Don't tell them how to work the program, tell them to let the process work. Tell them not to reject any help offered, don't close themselves off, and be unreachable. The staff, the medical personnel, the counselors are all there to help addicts get clean. They aren't there to beat them down, look down on them, or judge them. They are there to help. So let them.

And to the addict. Listen to the people who are trying to help you. You might think the questions are silly, not related to you or your situation, don't pertain to you, or whatever. Don't question the questions. Answer them. Answer them honestly and completely. Don't hold back. You'll only be doing yourself a disservice and hurt your chances of success. Another thing, don't think that the people trying to help you are stupid. They're probably not, and they've probably heard it or seen it before. So don't waste their time, or yours, trying to play games and trick them. Chances are it won't work, and it will likely lead to decreased chances of sobriety.

Some people enter rehab by their own choice. Some are "encouraged" by family. Some are given the option by a court or judge. Whatever takes you to rehab, you can succeed or fail. It's all up to you and the choices that you make. If you don't take the opportunity seriously and accept attempts to help, it's your choice and your fault when you fail. Like starting on the path that led to addiction, your choices define your future.

As I have mentioned, all rehabs are not the same. Some are legitimate, some, sadly, aren't. Like everything in life, you have to do your homework and make sure that the place you are going into is an honest, worthwhile facility. Some can be very helpful and help you achieve the sobriety that you want if you have the right attitude. Even if they have the potential to be what you need, they might have to be shown that you are serious about getting past your addiction. As I said, many people are in rehab for reasons that weren't their own and are only trying to pacify others. People who are in rehab for the wrong reasons, people that play games, can make it difficult for those that really want to beat the demon of addiction. Don't be belligerent about it, but don't stop trying to prove that you really do want to get clean, show them that you're serious. When they're sure you want real help, they will be there to provide it.

If one program or rehab isn't providing the help that you need, don't give up on the idea of rehab. Keep searching and researching until you find the right fit for you, the one that has the resources to help you in the way that you need. Just because you don't like pickles doesn't mean that nobody else does.

While it is reprehensible, there are facilities that promise help but only seek to use the addicts for their own gain. I know of some facilities that force their "patients" to work without pay, selling t-shirts or other items, promoting the facility, or something else, while providing no assistance to the addict to get sober. They promise counseling but don't deliver. But these facilities are not the only options. Some rehabs are, or claim to be, affiliated with a religious organization. Again, do your homework. They might be tied to an honest, legitimate religious organization or church. Or they could be using God's name to promote their agenda, but not following God's word. There are many documented cases of cults that claim to be churches but aren't. And there are rehabs that are part of a church that provide exactly what they promise. There are rehab organizations that genuinely care about their patients and provide everything that they can to help people beat their addictions and achieve sobriety. But even the best facility can only be as good as the addict is willing to let it be. A person who doesn't really want help, doesn't really want to get sober, can't be helped, no matter what is offered or how hard anyone tries. A person who does want to get clean, who will accept nothing less than a sober life, will never stop trying until they reach that success. Again, the choice is yours to make.

I have been told by addicts that have entered reputable, proven programs, that the counseling and group therapy sessions are a joke, stupid, useless, and don't do anything to help anyone. And I have told the addicts that said those things to me that if that is the way they approach it, that they are correct, it won't help them. Because they REFUSE TO LET IT. A hammer won't drive a nail if you don't pick it up. A car won't get you anywhere if you don't start the engine. And counseling won't help you find the answers that you seek, that you desperately need, if you don't believe that it can help and give it a chance. Counseling isn't a bad thing. It is a way to unlock things that are hidden in your subconscious. A counselor will ask questions, encourage you to talk about things. Sometimes uncomfortable things. Not to cause you pain, not to hurt you. But to help you work through problems and find solutions. To help let go of past pain, trauma, disappointment, or whatever it is, and make peace with it. So that it doesn't cause you more pain and anxiety, that is often an excuse to relapse. They aren't there to judge you. They are there to listen, to help interpret, and possibly guide you to a place where the pain doesn't hurt so much. If you aren't able to talk to a particular counselor, ask for someone else. Chemistry will be important in that it will help you build trust and open up. No matter who you end up talking to, there will be some uncomfortable conversations. You can't run from these. You can't hide from the truth of the past. But you don't have to live under the weight of the past either. Talking to someone, being open and completely honest, will help you get out from under that rubble and be able to look toward building something new, something stronger. Something sober. And remember, what you discuss with a counselor is between you and them. They aren't going to run and tell your family or friends what you said. They are not going to post it on social media. They are going to talk through it with you and help you find your way out of whatever jungle, maze, or hell you've been trying to escape.

But it's all up to you. You made the choice to start doing whatever it is you're addicted to. You have to decide it's time for a change. You will need help, but nobody else can make the choice to get sober for you. Nobody, no matter how bad they want to see you get clean, can do what it takes to get you there. Only you. Only your choices. Force doesn't often work.

Interventions, while usually done with the best intentions, can't make you make the right choice. Family, friends, some other outside force, can make you go through the motions. They can push you to enter rehab, give you no option but to get on the path. But only you can make it work. Only you can decide that it's time to put the bottle down, throw the needle away, stop whatever behavior it is that you think you can't live without and get clean and sober. Rehab can help you get there. But it's only a tool that you can use to help rebuild yourself. It's only as effective as you allow it to be. And it will only carry you to success if you truly want it to and allow it to.

Chapter 13: So, who am I hurting?

If you've been around an addict, you've undoubtedly heard this question. And if you are an addict, chances are you've asked it. Probably more times than you can count. This question is a go-to for addicts and is, most often, an attempt to deflect. We don't want to hear what we're doing wrong, how we're wasting our money, our lives, so we try to turn it around. We often make the argument that our substance abuse isn't doing them any damage. That if it is, we're the ones that will have to suffer the consequences, not the person trying to get us to stop. This question is a selfish attempt to get others to leave us alone, let us do what we want. And it is quite possibly the dumbest question I've ever asked or been asked. Who was I hurting? Well, let me tell you.

I'm going to tell you some things in this chapter that a lot of people that know me don't know about me. I'm going to describe in detail and complete honesty some of the drugs that I have done and the manner in which I did them. I'm not bragging. And I am damn sure not proud of any of it. But if you're going to understand, if you're going to recognize the gravity of what I'm trying to share, you need to know. I absolutely do not recommend anyone ever doing what I did, doing it how I did it, and sincerely hope that no one ever tries to reenact the stupid mistakes and choices I made. I'm really lucky to be alive. And that is not said for effect, pity, or exaggeration. It is the honest truth.

As I've already told you, I was raised by the best two people I have ever known. I was given a life that I didn't have to get. I was given a life that I probably didn't deserve. I know that for too many years, I didn't appreciate it, or the two people who gave it to me when they never had to. My parents were married for eight years before I came along. They had already established themselves in our hometown. They were small business owners. Respected by everyone that I ever knew. Genuinely good people. They didn't drink alcohol, never abused drugs. They were married for over fifty years and were always faithful to each other. The one thing that they wanted more than anything in the world, they couldn't have. A child. So, after years of trying, they made a choice. A choice that I'm sure tried their patience and probably made their hair grey before it should have been. They adopted me. That's what I mean when I say they gave me something that they did not have to give. I refer to them as my parents because that's what they were. They loved me as if I were their biological child. And I hurt them as badly as anyone could have.

I was, as I also said before, raised in church. I was given opportunities to learn many different things. Some of the family were farmers, and I learned a lot helping in the summers as I grew up. They gave me the opportunity to learn to play several musical instruments. That one, they might have wished they'd reconsidered when I got my first drum set. But they were supportive and encouraged me to learn, to question, to grow. They always pushed me to do the best job I could at anything I started. They taught me not to quit. They instilled in me a work ethic that would later become instrumental in both furthering my addiction and helping me escape it. They were always there for me when I needed them, and they never once let me down. I wish I could say the same thing.

You have already read about how my curiosity led me to substance abuse. I can say with every fiber of my soul that my parents never did anything to tell me it was acceptable. The truth is, they had told me that abusing alcohol and other things was wrong for as long as I can remember. I was told stories about "winos" in our hometown. I saw them, saw other people who had let substance abuse derail and ultimately destroy their lives. And I made a choice. I chose to try it anyway. I thought that I wouldn't get hooked, couldn't get caught up like that. I didn't know how wrong I was.

My slide into addiction was slow and steady. Many bad choices, many mistakes over many years. Until the demon finally decided I was in the right place to sink its claws. And they sank deep. My parents saw what was happening to me. And I argued with them. I told them they were wrong, that they didn't know what they were talking about. And yes, I asked them, "Who am I hurting?" More than once. A lot more than once.

They told me that I was hurting myself. That I would end up having health problems, that I could even die, if I didn't leave that stuff alone. I, like so many others before and after me, thought that I knew better and that "it can't happen to me." They told me

121

that I was wasting opportunities, like staying in college, that the drugs would bring financial struggles in the future. When I was in my teens, I didn't care about things like that. I was ten feet tall and bullet proof! They told me that I was hurting them, and I accused them of trying to use a guilt trip on me. And I wasn't addicted to anything and never would be. I was just having fun and asked again, "Who am I hurting?"

I made some other, shall we say, questionable choices. Using drugs for fun and excitement wasn't the only bad choice I made, but since this story is about addiction, we'll just stick with that. Like I said, I started and stopped over several years. I always worked. The work ethic that my parents had taught me, combined with them cutting me off financially when I got really stupid in my early 20s, allowed me to continue to survive and continue my downward spiral. The reason that they cut off any financial help wasn't related to my substance use, but that's a story for another time. Looking back, my exploration of recreational chemistry probably led to the choices I made that gave them no choice but to stop enabling me. And, also in hindsight, they were right about me not taking advantage of educational opportunities that would have allowed me to have better jobs, make

122

better money, and probably travel a different path. But I did make the choices. By myself. Nobody influenced me. In fact, many people told me I was crazy and should get my head on straight.

Isn't it amazing that sometime in our teens we decide that we know everything and that our parents, and everyone older, are stupid? Allow me a moment to digress here. I started thinking that around age 15, around the time I started experimenting with alcohol and drugs. I didn't realize until many years later that the truth was the other way around. They – my parents, "old people" – were right, and I was the stupid one. That was a hard pill to swallow, and I can honestly say, many years later, that I wish I had learned that lesson a lot sooner than I did. I apologize for getting off track for a moment, but I do believe that this is true and that others probably came to the misconception like I did. Through their desire to experiment with new, different things.

Anyway, back to what we were talking about. And please forgive me for repeating a lot of things. I repeat things I've already told you so that I can add context and deeper explanations. My first marriage started off fine, or so I thought. We were both pretty young and, as I just explained, had no real idea what life was like or how to make the most of it. We thought we had all the answers and that we'd live the "happily ever after" that everyone dreams of. We went our way, made our choices. And couldn't have gotten it much more wrong than we did. As the years went by, I did start to figure a few things out. One of those things was that I wasn't getting anywhere in the jobs that I had chosen. I got a little more education and joined my parents' business. I was clean again, had a daughter, and things started looking up. My second daughter joined us, and we were doing pretty well. Then I started getting comfortable and made the choice to start smoking marijuana again. That was the wrong choice to make. As I said before, it wasn't the only reason that marriage ended up failing, but I'm sure it didn't help. It was a choice that led to arguments, and I once again found myself asking, "who am I hurting?" I worked; all the bills were paid. I wasn't being unfaithful. I didn't see how I was hurting anyone. So, I didn't stop. I rationalized that I wasn't hurting anyone, I wasn't suffering because of it, so I didn't need to stop.

Other problems started popping up as they will do when unpleasant things are allowed to grow. And the combination of all of those things led to my first divorce. My daughters continued to live with me. And I have already told you how that went.

They saw me making bad choices, smoking marijuana, and being a generally bad father. But I refused to see that. I again asked who I was hurting. They had a home. They weren't going hungry. They had the things that they needed and a lot of what they just wanted. I was still working and moving up in a new job that had a very promising future. My parents tried to get me to see that I was making some mistakes. Ok, a lot of mistakes. But I told them they were wrong, that I knew what I was doing and that I had it all under control. But I was being controlled already and just didn't realize it.

Then I met my second wife, and the downhill slope I had been navigating got a lot steeper. Fast. Many people tried to blame her for what happened to me from this point. While she and I are not friends anymore and probably both agree that "we" should never have happened, I have never allowed anyone to place the blame for my cliff dive on her. And I still won't. I made the choices. I was my own problem and worst enemy.

As I told you before, after my first divorce I started playing in a garage band again. We played some bars and, while we were never going to be famous, we had fun and always had a lot of people come to watch us. We had a gig booked at a bar we hadn't played before and were packing everything so that we'd be ready to travel that weekend. I pulled something in my back and was on my knees. The pain was unreal, and I had trouble walking. This was early that week. Here's where I saw a horizon that I didn't realize was really a bottomless cliff, and that I was headed straight for it. The next day, I sent text messages to several people asking if they had anything that would help with the pain. Pain pills. I didn't send a group text; I sent them individually. And I sent a lot.

Unfortunately, several answered that they had one or two that they could give me. And none of them knew that I had asked and received the same answer from a number of others. I sure didn't tell them. All in all, I ended up with 35 opiate pain pills by that Friday morning. It was an assortment of some pretty powerful pills, oxycodone, hydrocodone, Percocet. The high dose varieties. I took 2 as soon as that friend gave them to me. I collected the others throughout that day. I took a couple more before the band loaded our equipment and a couple more throughout that night. We were scheduled to play Friday and Saturday night. I'll skip most of the details of that weekend because they aren't necessary, and to be honest, I don't remember all of that weekend. I know that the band played both nights. I was told that we put on a

126

really good show. I've seen some videos and pictures. Some of things that I don't remember.

I didn't even realize that I had done anything stupid or wrong until the next week. I had a friend that I would talk to as I drove to work. We were talking the next Wednesday morning, and I said something about it being Tuesday. My friend told me that I was mistaken, that it was, indeed, Wednesday. I had lost a day somewhere. I was stunned and, to be honest, scared. I asked a coworker later that morning if I had been at work all week. He looked at me like I was insane and told me that I had. And that I had seemed like me, like nothing was wrong.

I went back and counted the pills that night when I got home, and there were only four pills. I knew that I had started out with 35 the Friday before. And only had 4. I had taken 31 opiate pain pills over that weekend. That's what I meant when I said I'm lucky to be alive. I had been clean for a long time before that. Excluding marijuana and an occasional beer. But no opiates or hard drugs in many years. I told my doctor this story, and she told me that by all accounts, I should have died that weekend. I should have overdosed. By some miracle, I didn't. And, sadly, I wanted more. That craving had been reborn in a way

I never saw coming. And I really believe that was my moment of no return.

My second wife worked at that bar, and I met her for the first time that Friday night. After I had collected a prescription's worth of opiate pain pills, and started taking them. We didn't immediately start seeing each other, that came a few months later. That's why I won't blame her for my drug use, won't let anyone else point the finger at her. I'm not saying she was perfect, or even a good person, but no matter what else happened, she was not responsible for my getting strung out. I did that all by myself.

I didn't know, when I first met her, that she had a drug problem too. It never came up. Until we were hanging out with some of her friends. They had something that I'd never crossed paths with before. I knew about it, had heard horror stories about it. But when it was in front of me, my curious nature once again allowed me to make a bad choice. I met and was instantly addicted to methamphetamine. I knew better than to try it. I knew it was wrong. I even told myself that I was stupid to even consider it. Then I chose to do it anyway. Me. Nobody else.

That was when I reached that horizon I mentioned. And jumped without looking down. That was the moment the demon said, "you're mine" and I didn't even try to argue.

That marriage didn't last long. We were a disaster from the start. I just couldn't see through the drug haze to notice. I damaged my relationships with old friends, my parents, and my daughters. I was still asking, "Who am I hurting?" A stupid question. But a question with real answers that I was not able to see. That I chose not to see because I chose to give in to my addiction.

After that marriage dissolved, I continued to plumet toward an empty space that didn't seem to have an end. I had lost many friends. True friends that wouldn't accept or tolerate my drug use. I had strained the relationship with my parents. The two people who I respected most, who had loved me unconditionally. I hurt them and didn't even see that I had. My daughters pulled away from me and I couldn't understand why. Because I was lost to the substances, my addiction.

I told you earlier about the day I reached my personal rock bottom. The day I watched my youngest daughter being escorted into a court room. Because she had made bad choices. Because she had learned it from me.

Chapter 14: So now I know who I was hurting...

We've been skipping around, and we're not going to stop now. We'll come back to this place later, but I want to answer the question that we talked about in Chapter 13. It's a simple answer when you finally understand. I asked, and I'm sure many of you have asked or have been asked, "Who am I hurting?" The answer is everyone who cares about you.

When I was lost in my drug fueled nightmare, I didn't see that I was hurting everyone who cared about me. Friends, family, my daughters. I couldn't see through the fog to see the pain that I was causing. That I had argued with them about. That I had told them they were wrong about. It was real. And it was terrible.

My parents never gave up on me. They refused to give me money. They at least stood firm on that. And because they never gave up on me, they saw every step I took as I descended deeper into the clutches of my addiction. They saw the cuts, the blood, the scars that that demon left, and their hearts were broken because of it. My friends tried to talk sense into me, but I rejected them all, and they all eventually had to pull away from me. And my daughters. The two people who mean the world to me, that I made feel otherwise. I taught them that bad choices were acceptable. And, unfortunately, they followed a fool's example. I thank God that they were able to overcome their demons and are currently rebuilding their lives. While we try to rebuild the bridges that I burned those years ago.

I'll tell you more about how I got clean and the mess that was later. Now, I want to focus on the side that my parents saw, my daughters saw, and that many of you who love someone lost to addiction have seen.

When I told you the story about my youngest daughter, I told you that she slipped and started using again after our initial attempt to get away from drug abuse. I had managed to stay clean and had reached a new place in my life, a new understanding. When she started using again, I was devastated. I felt, and I believe I was correct in feeling, some of the responsibility. Because I had spent so many years demonstrating what I was watching her do. And it hurt.

We had many arguments during that time. I had learned a very valuable lesson from my parents. I wouldn't enable her. And that made her mad. Just like it had made me mad at my parents. But I held my ground and didn't give in. It eventually came to a head, and we had a huge fight. Things were said that don't need to be repeated here. Very hard and harsh words that left scars that we both still carry. And that we always will. We didn't speak to each other for about one whole year. I won't repeat her story. Instead, I'll tell you that I felt like I was largely to blame for her addiction. I know that it was ultimately her choice to do the things she did. But I couldn't shake the guilt that I had shown her that it was ok. And the pain I felt watching her go down the same path I did, being estranged, not talking to or seeing her, was worse than any pain I'd ever felt or imagined was possible.

I would wake up in the middle of the night and wonder if she was ok. If she was even alive. I couldn't reach her for a long time, had no idea where she was or how to contact her. I'd just lie there, not knowing. Staring into the dark. Afraid that I'd lost her. Maybe for good.

I realized during that time how my parents had felt. The agony, the fear. The questions that couldn't be answered. The pain that came from the words that cut so deep that it felt your life would bleed out. I'm not an emotional person, never have been. I have never been one to shed many tears over anything. But there were more than a few times when I broke down and just cried like a baby. Tears running down my face. And I couldn't make it stop. The pain, the fear, it was almost too much to bear. And the desperation of knowing that there was nothing I could do about it unless she made the choice to stop her self-destructive behaviors. My parents didn't have that knowledge. They had never stopped trying to get me to stop using drugs, trying to reason with me. Begging me to get away from drugs and the things I shouldn't have been doing. I knew something that they didn't. Because I am an addict and had been there myself. That no matter how bad I wanted my little girl to stop using drugs, to get clean, that it could never happen unless she made the choice herself. Nothing I could say, nothing I could do, that anyone could do, would make her stop. Until she was ready. And knowing that, knowing what she was doing, what could happen, almost drove me over the edge of sanity.

Those months of watching from this side, the clean side, made me understand exactly what my parents had seen. I finally knew why my friends had gone away. And it didn't feel good. I felt absolutely helpless, useless to help her. I had always brushed off everyone who tried to talk to me, to get me to get straight and clean. I never even considered how much pain and worry I was causing them. Being completely honest, I probably wouldn't have believed them if they had told me. I would have said they were exaggerating. But they weren't. I had to come through it all and be seeing it, living it from their side to finally understand.

My parents are gone now. It breaks my heart to know that I hurt them like I did, that I cut them so deeply. I am proud to say that they got to see me figure it all out. Finally. I was able to show them over a few years that I had beaten that addiction demon and that I would never go back. I couldn't take back the years of disrespect, the years of worry, the pain. But I will forever be grateful that they got to see me like they had before I made bad choices, got lost in all my mistakes. I thank God that they were able to see me as their son again.

And I am thankful also that my youngest daughter decided to take another lesson from me. She did what she had to do to beat her demon and is moving forward, growing stronger, and reaching higher every day. I can only guess that the relief, the gratitude, and the pride I feel is similar to what my mom and dad got to see. I promised them, along with my daughters and the friends that came back, that I would never make them see me fall again. My daughter promised me the same thing. We will hold each other to it.

Chapter 15: Destination: Rock Bottom

When discussing substance abuse and addiction, you often hear people talk about hitting rock bottom. People often wonder when the addict will reach that destination and figure out that they've got to change. But like addiction itself, rock bottom is not a specific spot on a map. It, also like addiction, is different for everyone. Some people find their rock bottom when they run out of places to go, people to help, and end up homeless. For others, it might be divorce. Loss of a good, stable job. And, sadly, for some, it is the ultimate rock bottom: death.

Cambridge online dictionary offers a few definitions of rock bottom. "The lowest possible level." "The most unhappy that someone has ever been in their life." "At the lowest possible level or in the worst situation." These are very accurate descriptions of what rock bottom feels like when someone finds themselves there. But how do you define your "lowest possible level"? Would your definition be the same for someone else? Does hitting rock bottom mean "the end"? Does it mean that there's no going back, no correcting course, and making things better? It doesn't have to.

Several online sources define rock bottom in another way. They tell the reader that rock bottom can be an opportunity. It doesn't have to be that everything is lost and that there's no going back. This thought process tells us that just because we have hit our lowest point, we can make different choices and turn everything around. It doesn't mean that no damage has been done. It doesn't mean that something never happened. It doesn't mean that your life will go back to being exactly like it was before. But it can get better. Some bridges get burned. Some are total losses. But others can be mended and serve as a connection again. It might not be the same as it was before, but it still functions and, over time, can prove that it can still bear any load that it ever carried.

I have seen several people that I know reach their rock bottom. But I'm not going to tell their stories here. I have seen homeless people. Some appear to be seeking a way to turn things around. Others seem content to stay where they are or find ways to go even lower. I'm not going to talk about them either. I'll tell you about my journey. I'll tell you how hard I looked for that elusive place, Rock Bottom, and about the crash I had when I found it.

As I've told you, I started out thinking I had all the answers, and I'd have no trouble living my life. And I've told you how wrong I was. I struggled and wandered around, taking different jobs and trying different avenues, but never found anything that would make life easy. That would pay me lots of money just because I thought I deserved it. I hadn't been raised to believe that. But I never fully grasped how hard life could be. I was never denied anything that I needed while I was growing up. I was taught that everyone had to work and do their part. That if you wanted something, you had to earn it. The part I didn't really get was that I didn't get to decide how much what I was doing was worth. I didn't understand that if I wanted to earn huge amounts of money that I would have to continue my education, make the necessary grades, and prove myself worthy.

Not that my parents didn't try to tell me. But, like I said before, they just didn't get it. I had it all figured out. Until I didn't.

Many questionable choices and actions led to me figuring it out. Not all related to my substance use and abuse, but I know that played a big role. You have probably heard the phrase FAFO – if not, look it up. Well, I found out. The hard way.

Another thing about me that I haven't shared is that I'm probably the most stubborn person I've ever met. That, like having a work ethic instilled in me, both helped and harmed. When I decided to move away from my childhood home, my parents wished me the best. And told me that they weren't going to pay for it. That if I was old enough to move out, move away, get an apartment that I was old enough to work and pay for it all. I didn't really expect them to pay for everything, but I certainly wasn't ready for the reality I was facing. I had never paid attention to their attempts to teach me about being responsible with money, how hard it could be to pay for everything that life required. Like most things, I let it go in one ear and right out the other. When I was struggling and didn't know if I'd be able to pay my rent, I asked for help. They said no. I was mad. But my stubbornness wouldn't let me admit defeat. I got a second job, then a better job, and crawled along the best way I could. I got by, but I didn't get ahead. And life sure wasn't like it had been when I was growing up.

A few short years went by. I married my first wife, and we continued the course we had been charting. Then our first child was coming, and I knew things had to change. So, I admitted that I had been mistaken about how easy it was going to be to take over the world and went crawling back to my parents. I didn't ask for money. I asked for a chance. They allowed me to get some education, get a certification, and join the family business. Things in my life improved. I got clean, my first daughter was born, and life was going pretty much like I thought it should. Then my second daughter was born. I made a decision to leave the family business and moved into another line of work. It had a lot of growth potential and was more suited to me and the work I liked to do. I've already told you how things were progressing through all of this, the return to occasional drug use and the bad choices and outcomes that followed, so I won't repeat that again.

So, we'll skip to where we left off before. I can remember very clearly the day that I crashed into my rock bottom. I've told you about that day at least a couple of times already. But sitting there in that court room, watching my daughter be brought in. Hearing the charges against her and the recommendation of the district attorney hit me harder than anything ever had before. I had been where she was before. More than once, I'm not proud to say. But none of those times ever slammed into me the way that seeing my daughter in that situation did.

The DA and my daughter's court appointed attorney had a deal already worked out. She was going to be sent to a boot camp for quite a while. The whole process was playing out, and I was helpless to do anything about it. I had already done my damage, shown her that what she did was acceptable when it wasn't. And there she was, being held accountable for her mistakes, but also, it felt, for mine. But then the judge did something unexpected. I told you how he stopped everything and asked me if I could handle her. How he called me out without being specific about it. How he released her to me and challenged me to fix my mistakes. So, again, I won't go into it again.

That was my lowest point. That was my ultimate rock bottom. But there had been many shelves in that pit. Maybe if I hadn't been stupid or blind, I'd have figured it out sooner. But I didn't. I hadn't even realized that I was digging that hole so deep. I had just kept my head down and kept trying to dig deeper.

I'll give you a quick overview of how things were so that I can show you how I started digging and how I refused to stop. I moved out of my childhood home at age 19. A friend and I got an apartment and were able to pay the bills and do pretty much what we wanted to do. We both worked. Everything was fine. He joined the military and started his new direction in life. I stayed in that apartment for a while, then my family helped me get a mobile home and set it on my parents' property. I still worked, but I started dabbling in drugs again and started the cycle of bad choices that would eventually lead me to leave again. I moved to another state. That's when the real Finding Out started for me. But I told you about that already. Fast forward to the job after I left the family business.

I was able to move up in that company and was able to make a six-figure income some years. And when I didn't hit the six-figure mark, I was always close. That lasted for several years. Until the company was sold. The new owners wanted to make changes, and I was ultimately separated and left with no direction. Sadly, during those few years, I had started to experiment with opiate pain pills, and other things, and I hadn't prepared for the place I found myself. My first wife and I had built a house, had purchased vehicles, had a lot of things that we hadn't needed but wanted. I wasn't able to find a comparable job, as the economy had taken a turn, and employment wasn't readily available. I ended up losing that house. By the time that happened, I was going through the death throes of my second marriage. I was depressed and used that, combined with the loss of my job, house, and everything else I had, as an excuse to continue to use and abuse drugs. I had alienated my family, most of my real friends. Even my daughters. And I was so far gone into the drug haze that I didn't even notice. At the time, I am ashamed to say, I really didn't care. I was all about "poor pitiful me" and mad at everything and everybody, and I didn't care. I just sank deeper and deeper onto the claws of the demon and stopped paying attention to anything else.

Before my headfirst dive off the stupidity cliff, I had bought a truck. It wasn't anything special. It was a little red Mazda. Four-wheel drive, dependable. I took care of it and had been proud of it when I was able to buy it on my own. It was paid for. It was all I had left after the fall. Then I was involved in an accident that totaled it. By pure luck, I was not at fault. I was hit by another vehicle. But my little red truck was gone. That was the last remnant of what I had had, that I had lost.

I borrowed an old van from my parents and drove it for a while. Someone at the church I had gone to as a child, that my parents were still very much a part of, gave them an even older van to give to me. I had gone in a couple of very short years from six figures, home, family, to maybe I had a job, living in an old hand-me-down van sometimes, with family that might know where I was. But most of the time, they didn't. My daughters had gone to live with my parents. I stayed with whoever would let me, a motel if I had the money, or slept in the van. And still found ways to get drugs. And kept doing drugs.

That's when I got the phone call telling me my daughter had been arrested and was looking at being sent to that boot camp. I cleaned myself up as well as I could and went to her court hearing. You know what happened then.

A family member had a house that was empty and offered to let me and my daughters move into it. If I would commit to getting and staying clean and find steady, stable employment. I agreed to those terms because, like I said, I had crashed and burned that day in that court room. It wasn't easy, it was very humiliating and painful. But I made a choice to stop choosing wrong. I made the choice to choose right and take my life back.

That was my rock bottom. That was my lowest point. It took time. It wasn't easy. But I somehow made it through. It was a long, hard, emotional, painful process. There were many times I thought I couldn't make it. A few times, I almost gave up. I have not told many people this, but it is true, and it did happen. I reached a point where I felt everything was lost, that there would never be a way back. I wrote "the note." I kept it hidden, never told anyone about it. Never gave it to anyone. And, as I hope you have figured out, I never acted on it. But I was so close. We'll talk more about that later.

I finally understood what rock bottom was. I finally knew what real, severe depression felt like. I finally saw what it looked like to have no place, no plan, and no future. I looked in the mirror and I did not like who I saw. I hated that person. I despised that man and thought that he was the worst example of a man I'd ever seen. He was a terrible father. He had failed twice as a husband. Had lost jobs and couldn't find, and didn't deserve, anything like the jobs he'd had. He'd broken the hearts of his parents, the best people he'd ever known. His friends were all gone. The real friends. Not the good time, get high party "friends," they were still willing and wanting to be there. But the true friends that cared, that hurt when they saw him making the self-destructive choices, were gone. The ones that had to leave him. I looked in the mirror and told that man he shouldn't be alive. That he certainly didn't deserve pity. Or "help." He deserved everything that had happened to him. Because he had chosen it. He had made choice after choice after choice to get here. And that he was depressed and sad and pitiful was his own damn fault. I saw a man that was ready to give up completely.

And that's when I told that man that things were going to change. I didn't know how. I had no idea where to start or how to turn things around. But I got rid of "the note." I stopped making excuses, stopped allowing myself to accept the excuses I was making. I decided then that I would stop making bad choices, no matter how hard it was or what I had to do. I made the choice to change.

Chapter 16: Another long journey began

Like I said, I had no idea how to make things better. I had no real job, no money. I was barely scraping by doing odd jobs when I could find them. I was alone. I had isolated myself from everyone who loved me, insulated myself in bad choices and countless mistakes. I had no one to turn to. But I had to start somewhere.

I called my dad. I didn't ask him for anything. Except to listen, and to give me a chance. He listened. I told him that I was sorry. That I knew how pitiful it was to say it, and how I knew that it didn't take away all the bad things that I had done, all the pain I had caused. But that I knew then that he was right about everything. Everything he had tried to teach me, that I had rejected. Every opportunity I had passed by. That I was not going to be that man anymore. He told me that I was a good person. Of course a dad would say that. I told him that I knew he was just saying that, but that I could be. I could be the son that he and my mom had raised. That I could make something out of the rubble I had created. I told him that day that I would be back.

After that conversation, that very humbling and painful conversation, I reached out to another person. An old friend, possibly my longest standing friendship. I reached out to one of the best friends I'd ever had, the friend that had always been there. The friend that had tried to talk me out of some of my worst choices. The friend that had been my babysitter when I would experiment with substances I should never have tried. The friend that had eventually had to walk away.

He answered. And he listened too. He told me that he wanted to believe me. That he wanted to see me do the things I told him I was going to do. But that I would have to show him. That my words weren't enough. And, most importantly, that he'd give me the chance to prove it. I asked him to hold me accountable, to call me out if I did anything that seemed wrong, like I was going in the wrong direction again. He said he would. And he kept his word. Sometimes rather harshly. I made him a promise that I was going to beat my demon, overcome addiction, and never be that person again. He made me a promise, too. That he would hold me to that promise even if he had to beat sense into me. I'm glad it never came to that because I'm sure he would have. But he didn't give up on me. He didn't shut me out. He had reached a point where he wouldn't allow me to manipulate him, he wouldn't enable me anymore, and he wouldn't watch me destroy myself years earlier. But he was still willing to see if I would keep my word and make the choice to get it right. I had no right to ask him. He had no obligation to do it. But he did.

I contacted another friend and had the same conversation. With the same result. I had two friends from my past, from when I was making better choices and doing things as I should have been, that were willing to see if I could ever get back to that place. Neither was going to do it for me. Neither was going to do anything other than wait and see. And be there if I needed to talk, someone to lean on, or someone to stop me if I started toward the dark again. They were willing to be a safe place, a place to be vulnerable but not punished. They didn't judge me. They didn't tell me how I had hurt them; how stupid I had been. They never said, "I told you so." They didn't have to. They were just the true friends, the good people that I needed to help me stay focused and get my life together.

It did not happen overnight. It took a long time. Any real recovery will take time and effort. A lot of both. I have repeatedly said throughout this rambling story that detoxing is very difficult and very dangerous. I have said every time that anyone that is going to go through that needs to seek medical advice and be helped, coached, and monitored while they are getting the substance out of their bodies. Detoxing is hard on many levels. It drains you physically. It is painful, very painful. And, as I have told you before, it can be lethal. I have read many stories of people who died while going through detox. If they had reached out for help, if they had gotten medical professionals and others involved, it might have been different. They might have survived and be here today. It is emotionally painful. Facing the truth of the destruction that you have caused, the pain you have caused, and the guilt you carry for all of it can be devastating. It can be too much and can lead to relapse. Or worse. Seeking help, counseling, advice from people who are trained to help you confront and work through these emotions is not wrong. It isn't always pleasant, but it is the right thing to do. Trying to face all of the bad things that we have done alone is probably another disaster waiting to happen. Don't let what you fear others will think stop you from seeking whatever help you need, any help that is available, and anything that will help you make the right choices. Don't try to do it alone.

I did. And I somehow survived. I detoxed for several days. I was sick. I honestly thought I was going to die. My friends, my parents, and my daughters kept watch, and I know they would have called for help if things had gotten worse than they did. I talked to my friends and my dad a lot. I talked to them and told them what I would have told a counselor. It was very hard, being open and honest with them. Telling them things that could have made them walk away. But I made myself do it. And they didn't walk away. They just let me talk and work it out. And over several months, I got better.

Some people did stay away. Some of the friends I had before I went off the deep end refused to come back. They wouldn't give me another chance. Some family members felt that way, too. No matter what, they were not going to let me back into their lives. They had the right to make whatever decision they wanted. It hurt, in some cases, but I had to respect their decisions. I couldn't blame them for not wanting to risk being let down or hurt again. I couldn't lash out at them and blame them for choices I had made that led to betraying their friendship. I could only tell them that I was sorry for everything that had happened and allow them to go on with their lives. I suppose I could have been bitter, could have harbored resentment toward them. But it would have been wrong. It would have been unfair. Just like it was wrong and unfair to hurt them, betray their friendship, and trust. I had made the choice that I wasn't going to be a part of their lives before because I chose drugs. I really had no right to question them, to blame them for continuing to live the lives they had made without me. Another place where my bad choices would affect the rest of my life. But my choices had been mine. I made them. And I had to accept the consequences of my choices and respect the choices that they had made.

I was still at my lowest point. I had nothing but that van and some clothes. The economy was still recovering, and work was still hard to find. Especially when I had been in corporate management before I dove off that cliff. I had many interviews and was told that I wouldn't be happy with the jobs that were available because of my background. I heard that many times. I went to an interview that a friend had recommended, and was told the same thing by the owner of that company. I'd had enough. I had to work. I had to start somewhere. So, I told him that if he needed a ditch dug, give me a shovel. I told him that while I had been pretty far up the ladder before, I had no problem starting on the ground again. That if the opportunity to climb the ladder existed, that's all I needed. I would start out on the ground and prove that I was worthy of climbing back up. I did actually say that about the ditch and the shovel. He decided to give me a chance, and a job. And it was at the bottom.

And I was glad to have it. I started that job immediately. The pay was close to one third of what I had earned before. I didn't particularly like that part, but I accepted that it was what I had to do. Because of choices I had made. So, I started and worked. I didn't complain about it; I didn't seek pity. I was in the situation I was in because I had made choices to be there. And I made choices to learn everything about the job, the work, the company. And I started climbing. When I reached the highest point at that company, I made a choice to look at other opportunities. I wanted more, I wanted to go higher, so I looked for a larger company with more room to climb.

I met the woman who would become my third wife after I had been clean almost one year. Her brother-in-law is the friend that suggested I apply where he worked, that led to the ditch and shovel interview. I keep talking about the ditch and shovel because it really is significant. Once you've thrown everything that ever mattered, that had value, and the people who cared about you away, you have very few choices available. You have to accept that you are where you put yourself. Back at the bottom. And you have to prove yourself all over again. You can't expect people to just start trusting you again, believing that you will be responsible and do things right, and hand it all back to you. No. You have to earn it all again. Is it fair? Absolutely. You made the choices to risk everything. You made the choices that led to losing everything. So, yes, you absolutely deserve to be doubted and have to work harder than you ever did before to earn your way back. That might be a hard pill to swallow, but it's a lesson worth learning. And if you don't accept the responsibility for being back at the bottom, you will probably end up staying there.

Anyway, the woman that would become my third wife had dealt with addicts most of her life. And

154

she was tired of it. She was very up front about her feelings about alcohol and drug use from the first time we talked. She made it very clear that she didn't have to ever live that life again and that she wouldn't. She told me that if I ever started acting like my old self that she would walk away and not look back. That if I couldn't stay clean that she wouldn't watch me destroy myself. That might sound harsh, demanding. But she was justified to say it. And she would have been right to walk away if I hadn't kept my word and stayed clean. Some might see that as an unfair ultimatum, words from someone who didn't care enough to be supportive and help me through the hard times. Some might call her selfish and say that she didn't really care about me. They would all be wrong.

Our first year together was hard. I was still working on getting clean. Like I said, it's not an overnight process. The cravings don't just disappear like smoke in the wind. They hang around and keep trying to whisper, keep trying to sing a lullaby that will bring you back into their embrace. The memories linger, and the desires hang around too. Always trying to get you to open the door so that they can come back in. Like every couple, we had our ups and downs. I could have communicated more effectively if I had known how. I knew that I was struggling, but I didn't know how to express it. I was still learning how to stay clean, still learning how to fight my demon. At times I would pull away, or push her away, and try to internalize everything. I wouldn't tell her, or anyone else, that I was having a hard time. That I was wondering if I was going to be able to hold on and win that war. But I did stay clean, I didn't give in to the cravings and urges. We made it through our first year, and things started to get better. The cravings were not as bad. They were actually starting to disappear. I had someone that loved me, that gave me a reason to stay focused on the future. She never understood how important that was. Her belief that I could win the war, that I could banish my demon forever. And I didn't know how to tell her. I hadn't figured that out yet. I still had a lot to learn and a long way to go. But I was determined to get there, to succeed.

My parents were getting older and needed help maintaining their property. I started going and helping take care of their yard and doing whatever I could to help them. My dad and I spent many afternoons picking up tree limbs and sticks, burning yard debris, and just talking. Finally. I had spent too many years not talking to him, too many years being a stupid kid who wouldn't listen. Then too many years being too strung out on drugs to listen. I couldn't make up for those years. But I tried to make the most of the time I had then. One day while we were working in his yard, he told me that he was sorry for the times he had refused to "help" me, for cutting me off financially, and for being critical of the choices that I had been making all those years before. It caught me by surprise. I didn't expect anyone to apologize to me for the stupid mistakes I had made, for not allowing me to take advantage of them.

I didn't think. I didn't wait. I told him "Don't be." I told him that he had nothing to apologize for and that he should never feel any amount of guilt or doubt about the things he had done and said to me. I told him that he was right to do the things that he had done; to cut me off, to leave me to the consequences of my choices, to let me learn about life the hard way. I thanked him. I realized at that moment, when he tried to apologize to me, that he had done me the greatest favor that anyone had ever done in my life. He had been the first one to hold me accountable. I didn't realize it then, certainly didn't admit it, and change my behaviors. But he had told me "No." He had drawn a line and wouldn't back down. Yes, I was stubborn and ran away, made my bad choices, and tried to prove that he was wrong. But I hadn't proven him wrong. I had proved that he was right all along. I told him that while it didn't show, the lessons that he had taught me – work ethic, right and wrong, all of if – had been the foundation of what I needed to climb out of the hole I had made of my life. He still tried to tell me that he wished he had been more supportive, had helped me along the way. I told him that I was the one digging my hole. I told him that when I hit rock bottom, if he had offered to help, had come to me, I would have only asked for a pick and shovel so I could dig that hole deeper. I told him that by standing his ground, by holding true to his values and his word, that he had shown me that only I could fix me. That I had to make the choice. That I had to put in the work. That no matter how bad he had always wanted to see me get things right, only I could make it happen. And that enabling me would have only let me think that I was making good choices, would have allowed me to prolong the inevitable. That he would have only given me ammunition to hurt him, my mom, and everyone else more and longer. I told him he had no reason to ever apologize to me. I had every reason to apologize to him, and everyone else. That I had been the one to make mistakes. That not enabling me was NOT a mistake, but the only right thing to do.

I made him a promise that day. I promised him that no matter what happened, no matter what life threw at me, I would never again allow myself to become who I had been. That I would stand up, face whatever came sober and clean. That I would do whatever I had to do to figure things out and be successful. I swore to him that I would never again use drugs. I have kept that promise. I will never break it.

My parents loved the life I was rebuilding. They loved the woman I was with, was going to marry. My mom suffered from dementia, but she had the chance to see me get clean and start living the life I always should have. My wife and I got married the year that I lost my parents. My mom had good days and bad days. On one of her good days, she asked my wife to take care of her boy; me. My mom and dad both told me that they were proud of me, proud to see that I had started making the right choices and was on my way to being who I was supposed to be. They both got to see it happen for a few years. Not enough years, not nearly as many years as they had had to watch me getting it wrong. But they did get to see, to know that I was on a better path and wasn't going to allow myself to fail again. My proudest achievement, the one thing that I will be forever thankful for, is that they were both given the opportunity to see that their lessons, their love and support, their belief in me were not going to be wasted. That the person who had caused them pain, had let them down, was gone. That the son they had tried to raise had finally become who they knew he could be. I still live with the guilt, knowing the pain and disappointment I caused them. But I did get the chance to tell them that I was sorry, and that I appreciated them and loved them more than I could ever show them. That their love, their support, and belief in me, combined with the same from my wife, had been the rock, the foundation that allowed me to make it through. That they had been instrumental in my winning the war with drugs. I don't know what I would feel if I hadn't been able to get it right in time for them to see, to know. I thank God that I don't have to know, that he allowed me the opportunity to show them before they went home.

Chapter 17: Time for some hard truth

I've told you my story. I didn't drag it out, and I kept it focused on my addiction, my history. I've given you my opinion about addiction in general, some of the things that every addict does, and also some things that those that love addicts do as well. And, like I said on the first page, I haven't pretended to be anything I'm not, haven't tried to portray myself as some expert. I've shared things here that very few people knew about. A couple of things that no one knew about. My reason for doing this is a hope that I can help someone, anyone who is an addict, anyone that loves an addict, or someone who just wants to see it from a real person's perspective.

Now I just want to give you my advice. Again, I'm not a doctor. I'm just someone who made a lot of bad choices, but with God's help, and the love of some family and friends, figured it out. Some of what comes next might hurt. You might not agree with what I have to say. But it is the truth as I understand it, as I have lived it. I do not want to offend or hurt anyone, but I know I would be leaving this unfinished if I stopped here.

Whether you're an addict who wants to beat addiction or someone who loves an addict and wants to see them get sober, there are things that I want to say that I believe with all my heart will help you. Getting sober is a process, and it is a painful one. Watching someone struggle with addiction is just as painful. I have lived both sides. Everything that I have written, I have told people in my life. People who were addicts or were trying to understand addiction, to help an addict that they loved. I did read and research a lot. I spent years learning about addiction as I was fighting my way to sobriety. I have talked to friends, co-workers, and strangers. I even had a doctor ask me to try to explain addiction. The doctor asked me to talk about it because I refuse to ever take another opiate pain pill or shot. For any reason. I tell all my doctors now on my first visit that I am an addict and to put in all capital letters on the top of my chart "NO OPIATES FOR ANY REASON." I don't do that to brag or pat myself on the back. I tell them because I don't trust myself to allow it back into my body. If I get hurt, and I have, I just have to deal with it. That's the only choice I have now. The only choice I will make now.

I have also told you that I don't think I'm better or smarter than anyone else. I don't think I'm some kind of hero. I just know that I have lived a life, had experiences, that might help someone find a way to sobriety.

Having said that, I want to speak directly to each side. The addict and the one trying to help an addict. Because I have been both. I'm not trying to say that my way is the only way, or even that it's the right way. I'm saying it worked for me. Maybe, hopefully, it will help you find your way to the right path for you.

Chapter 18: A few words for an addict

If you're an addict and you're reading this, it must mean that you want to be sober. I, like your family and friends, sincerely hope that you want that. And that you find it. It won't be easy. It won't be quick. You will feel pain like you have never felt. You will have scars. But if you really want to be clean, if you really want to be sober, it will all be worth it. It might seem that I'm being hard on you. I am. Because I was hard on myself. And you will have to be too. You will struggle. You will want to quit. You will think you can't do it, that no matter what, you're going to fail. Getting sober isn't for the weak. It takes strength. Strength of will, of spirit, and a desire to be the better version of yourself that you know you can be. Your demon won't just let you go. You will have to fight. You will have to keep going when you think you can't. Getting clean and sober is possible. And anyone who wants it badly enough can get it. But know this, and don't forget it. Only you can fix you. That is, in my opinion, an absolute truth about overcoming addiction. You, and only you, can fix you.

I have been where you are. I am telling you what I believe to be an absolute truth. Only you can fix you. You have to want it. You have to want it so desperately that you will stop at nothing to get sober, to get clean, to stop the self-destruction. You can't use anyone, can't hurt anyone, and can't expect anyone to do it for you. It's all on you. You made the choices that got you here. It's up to you to make different choices, better choices. Only you can fix you.

But there are some things that you must do that can't be avoided. I believe that the first step on the journey to sobriety is admitting that you have a problem. That's pretty universal in all of the programs I have read about. And it is absolutely correct. It can't be that your mother told you that you have a problem.

Or your friends. Or your spouse. It has to be you. You have to see it for yourself and admit it to yourself. I told you how I looked at myself in the mirror and got mad at the person looking back at me. Because he wasn't the "me" I was supposed to be. He was the weak "me" that allowed drugs to take over, to be in charge. I had denied my addiction, to my family and friends, but to myself too. I had lied to myself and thought that I was in charge, that I was in control. I wasn't. And you aren't either. If you think you are, you're wrong. You have to be able to see the truth, the absolute naked truth, and not turn your eyes away. You have to accept what you have allowed yourself to become. And you have to understand that it doesn't have to be this way. It doesn't have to define who you will be for the rest of your life.

And you're going to have to change more of your behaviors than just drinking, doing drugs, or whatever it is that you're addicted to. Getting sober isn't easy. Add everything else, and it might seem overwhelming. But you can't try to take shortcuts. You can't do it halfway. It's all or nothing. I'll talk about some things, in no particular order, that I have seen and lived through. I'm sure there are many more, but I can only talk about what I've experienced.

Let's start with Pride. The story I told about getting a job because I told the owner of a company that if he needed a ditch dug to give me a shovel is absolutely true. I went, as I told you, from a job making six figures most years to barely above minimum wage. You don't think that was quite humbling? It was. I will not lie and say that I wanted to have to start at the bottom again. I would have loved to be handed a job that paid what I wanted, that was like what I had thrown away. But that's not how life works. I had to swallow my pride and understand that I had put myself in that position. That the choices I had made had brought me down to that place. And you have to understand that the choices you made have brought you to where you are. You can't say that you're too good to do a certain job, perform menial tasks. You can't say that you're better than that. You can't say that you can't take orders or direction from someone else who might not have as much experience as you do. If you've lost yourself to addiction, you really don't have anything to be proud of. If you're at rock bottom and you have nowhere to turn, what do you have to be proud of? You have to accept that you made choices that caused you to lose whatever it is that you lost. A job, a house, a spouse. You could have been a CEO, the big boss. And lost it all through your addiction. And found yourself homeless, penniless, wanting nothing but your next beer or your next fix. It doesn't have to be that extreme. If you have made choices that took everything away from you, everything you had worked for, every relationship you had built, every dream you had, what, at that point, would you have to be proud of? I'm not trying to beat you down or make you feel worse about your situation. But I'm being honest. Pride isn't something that you can have at this point. So, if you have to start over, start at the bottom again, that's what you have to do. It doesn't have to mean that you'll always be at the bottom. You started there once and climbed higher, didn't you? So do it again. Be grateful for the opportunity, whatever it is, and make the most of it. Be the best you can be. It doesn't matter what it is. Do it to the best of your ability. And do it with pride. That you are working your way back up is something that you CAN be proud of. Don't go around bragging about it. Just do it and let your achievements show on their own. People will notice. They don't need you to tell them about it. They need you to show them. You showed them how to make bad choices, screw everything up, and lose everything. Now you have to show them that you are serious about getting things right. That you will do whatever it takes. Don't spoil it by bragging and saying, "Look at me, look at me!" If you do what you are supposed to do, they will see it. And they will be proud of you, too.

Understand, too, that you aren't entitled to anything. The only person who owes you anything is you. If all you have done is use people, manipulate them, and take advantage of them, they aren't going to be too willing to hand you anything. You can't expect your family or friends to provide you with a place to live, a car, job, or anything. They might be willing to offer a little help. You might think it should be more. You might think that they're punishing you, trying to hold you down, keep you from getting back on your feet. You'd be wrong. It's not their place to give any of those things to you. It's your job to earn them. It's your responsibility to do whatever it takes to get the things that you need. Notice that I did not say the things that you want. You can't start there. You have to start with the necessities, the things that you need to survive. You need shelter. It could be that someone offers you a place to stay while you work on getting your life back together. It could be that no one trusts you enough to invite you to live in their home. You might have to find a homeless shelter. A place where you have a bed to sleep in, a place to take showers, wash your clothes. Maybe they have a meal program, maybe not. If that's all that is available, you take that and you make it work for you. Remember what I said about pride? You can't be too proud, too good, to do anything. You have to do whatever you can, take any resources that are available, and make the most of them. I have worked with people who lived in homeless shelters for a few months while they saved money to get an apartment. Some were serious about making a better life for themselves and were able to start rebuilding their lives. I have also known people who went to a shelter but didn't do anything to make their situation better. They used it as a place to stay off the streets while they waited for someone else to come along and do it for them. None of those ever worked out. They felt that someone should allow them to move into their home or pay rent for them to have their own apartment. They felt that they were entitled to that, and more. They were very wrong. They weren't entitled to anything but a chance to prove that they wanted sobriety and a better life than what they and their own choices had created. If you aren't willing to put in the work, the effort, to make your life better why should anyone else? Why should your friends or family work themselves into the ground, put in extra hours, get a second job just to hand money over to you when you aren't willing to do it for yourself? They shouldn't be willing to. And you shouldn't expect anyone to.

Which brings me to another point, one often tied to entitlement mentality. Don't make demands. Of anyone for anything. You aren't entitled to that either. You can ask. They can say no. If they do, you have to accept it. But never go to anyone demanding money, a ride, or anything. You made choices that took things from you. It's never good to demand anything in the first place. But if you've made choices that destroyed your life, your former happiness, and damaged others, you most certainly can't believe that you're in a position to tell anyone what they have to do or to give you. So don't do it. The only demands you can make at this point are demands of yourself. Demand that you stop the self-destructive behaviors. Demand that you stop drinking alcohol, using drugs, or whatever it is that you chose to become addicted to. But do not try to pressure anyone, don't try to manipulate anyone, and do not demand that anyone do anything.

And never steal from anyone. You made choices that cost you everything. They didn't. They have worked for what they have, and you have no right to any of it. If they choose to give you something, be grateful. Because they certainly don't

171

have to. If they won't give you something, that is their right, their choice. You have to accept it and respect it. You don't steal. Period.

Stop thinking you're a victim. You are, but of your own making. The world, your family, your friends, your employer, none of them made your choices. You did. So, if you are a victim, you're your own victim. Don't try to play victim to make people feel sorry for you or give you things. That is manipulation. And that has to stop. All of your old addict games have to stop. And most addicts are so accustomed to playing the victim that they let it continue into their search for sobriety. It can't continue because it's nobody's fault but yours. So, just stop it. Don't play the self-pity games either. That's pretty much the same thing. Yes, you feel like you have let everyone down, disappointed them and yourself, and have probably lost, wrecked, or destroyed everything that ever meant anything to you. And, yes, that is a pitiful situation. But it's no one else's fault. It's yours. Because you made bad choices. It is terrible to be in that place, I know, because I have been there too, but we only have ourselves to blame. But you can't waste time wallowing in self-pity or expecting pity from others. If that's all you do, you'll never break free and find a sober life. You'll lose yourself again and, most likely, end up back where you don't want to be. Yes, you screwed everything up. Yes, you made a huge mess of your life, and possibly other lives. Yes, you feel bad about everything you did, every bad choice you made. And you should. But you can't let it consume you. You have to acknowledge all of it. You can't deny it. You can't run and hide from it. You have to face it. You. Not your family, not your friends, not the world. You. Constantly, or even occasionally, throwing pity parties won't ever push you to success and a sober, clean life.

You must accept your responsibility. You have to admit to your part, that you and the choices you made brought you to where you are. Don't waste your time, or anyone else's, making excuses for any of it. Face it honestly. Admit it all. To yourself mostly. Most of us have a hard time admitting when we make a mistake. Let alone a series of mistakes that end up taking everything away from us. But it has to be done. Believe me, I didn't want to do it. I told you what I felt when I looked at myself in the mirror. I told you how I despised the man I saw looking back at me. I don't think I've ever been more mad at someone in my life. And I only had me to blame. I had a serious "come to Jesus" meeting with myself. It was very difficult and very painful. I thought back over the years that I had spent lost in a drug haze and tried to remember every stupid, wrong choice I had made. I'm sure that I missed a lot because I was so out of it. But I tried to remember everything. My brain didn't want to help. It kept trying to throw "good," "fun" memories in to throw me off track. But I knew that those memories, memories of "good times," were all false. I, like you, thought that I was having fun and really living a great life when I was using drugs. You can deny that if you want to, but denial won't help you. But after I got clean, after I got my head straight, I realized that all of those so-called "good times" were lies. Those were the times I was teaching my daughters that being strung out and irresponsible were acceptable. Those were the times when I didn't make sure all the bills were paid. I had to look at all of it with sober eyes, a clear head, and admit that all of it had been wrong. I had to accept that I had made many horrible choices and that when they were all added together, it equaled disaster. For my life, my daughter's lives, my parents' lives. I had caused so many people so much pain. And I could never take it back. I felt guilt like I had never known. And you should, too. You should feel guilty about the damage that your choices have caused. To yourself and to those that cared about you. And you should face each and every one of the disasters that you caused. You should be honest about everything. To yourself, or to a therapist if you need help processing and understanding it. And as I've said over and over, asking for help isn't a bad thing. It can be a good thing. We all need someone to talk to, to help us make sense of the jumble in our heads. And for addicts, we need to learn how to think straight again. We need to know that there is a way out. It doesn't make you weak to talk to someone. But if you do, you absolutely have to be honest. You can't lie. You can't hold back. You have to admit everything and accept responsibility for everything you did. If you don't accept full responsibility for the choices you made and the results that those choices lead to, you won't find your way out. You won't be able to beat your demon. You won't find sobriety or happiness.

Another thing you'll have to accept is that your old life, before you got lost to addiction, isn't going to come back. Not like it was. Wounds can heal, but they leave scars. Scars fade over time, but they never go away. I lost a lot of friends because of the choices I made. As you probably have, too. Some, a very few, of those friends were willing to give me a chance to show them that I was going to get clean, that I wasn't going to be that person anymore. Many more weren't.

I could say that they were never really my friends if they wouldn't give me a chance. I could be bitter about it and blame them. But I would be dead wrong. They all had to make choices, too. And deciding that they weren't willing to watch me be strung out and acting a fool was a choice that most of them made. And they walked away from me. As they should have. I would have only brought them down with me. I told you about two long-time friends that were the first two that I reached out to. I was lucky because they still cared enough about me to at least give me a chance to show them. They didn't trust me. They had no reason to. There have been other friends that have come back over the years. After I proved myself. After I kept my word and wouldn't let myself fall back into my old routines. But there are many more that turned away and never looked back. They haven't and probably never will. It doesn't mean that they are bad people. It means that I hurt them, that I destroyed something, and that it can't be fixed. It doesn't make me happy, doesn't make me feel good. But it is my fault because I made choices that left them few choices, or no choices at all. I hold no grudges, no anger, no bitterness because they didn't choose to let me back into their lives. I have to accept that they did what they had to do because of what I chose to do. I have to live with that. I can't, and don't, blame them for it. I respect their choices. You have to do that too. You can't be mad at anyone who won't allow you to come back into their life. You had your chance, as I did. And you, just like me, blew it. Be grateful for the ones that did give you another chance. Never begrudge any that didn't. That goes for family, too. Some people think that family should forgive anything. I'm not one of those people. I know that they have feelings and that if they are hurt badly enough, they will walk away too. They have to. To protect themselves and be able to live their lives. We don't have to feel good about it, certainly don't have to like it. But we have to accept that, too.

Then there are people who don't need to come back into your life. I'm sure you know exactly who I'm talking about. The "good time" friends that you got drunk or high with. The ones who accepted your bad choices, encouraged them even, that went right down that path to Hell with you. They might have disappeared when you started on the path to sobriety. They might have thought you'd be back, that you'd fail. And they might try to come back while you're still making that journey. They might not try to get you to go drinking with them. But the memories will be there, and they will try to break you down, tempt you, lead you back to the wrong places and wrong choices. If they are still engaging in whatever substance you shared, the demon will be calling to you. Being around those people will slow, will probably stop, your progress. You shouldn't hate them. You shouldn't be mean, rude, or hateful to them. You should simply tell them that you are going in a different direction and can't go back to that life. And since they want to keep living that life, you can't be around them. Be honest. Don't make excuses to avoid them. Tell them that you are going to get clean, going to get sober, and get back on track to the life you were supposed to live. And that you're not going to let anything stand in your way. Don't judge them. You have no right to. Just move on with your life. Without them.

And one last thing. This might be hard for you to do, it might be humiliating or painful. But it is something that you have to do. You owe it to yourself, but you owe it to the people you hurt more. You have to apologize. Not just words, not just a quick, meaningless empty lie. A sincere, deeply honest, and heart-felt apology. You might not even remember the details or know the extent of what you did to them. But they do. I know that it was one of the hardest things I ever did. My first apology was to my daughters. The three of us sat together, and I talked.

I told them that I knew I didn't remember everything and probably didn't even realize some of the things that I did that hurt them. I did know a lot of what I had done and laid it all out. I didn't try to shortcut anything. My second marriage had hurt them deeply. I knew that that woman and I had both treated them badly and unfairly. I knew that I had been an absent father for a long time. I knew that I had let them see me doing drugs and acting like a complete idiot. I asked them to tell me things that I had done that had hurt them. I encouraged them to be open, to be completely honest about all of it. They did. And it hurt. It was like being punched over and over and over. But I knew I deserved it. When all of the cards were on the table, I simply told them that I was sorry. That I knew that that didn't take any of the things that I had done or the pain away. But that I really did know that I had screwed things up, and that I was genuinely sorry. And promised them that I would never let any of it happen again. I had a conversation with my parents. With my closest friends. With other family and friends that didn't believe me and wouldn't give me another chance. I didn't get mad at them. Not any of them for anything they told me. I had to accept what I had done, and I did. I was truly sorry for all of it, and I owed each and every one of them an apology.

I couldn't give them an explanation. I hadn't had time to figure it out. I didn't know how to put it into words yet. But I did tell them that I was sorry. I'll come back to this later, but the important thing is that you do it. Don't do it if you don't mean it. Don't do it if it's not real and sincere. Don't lie, don't pretend. But you do owe it to everyone. Even yourself.

I guess you might be feeling a little beaten up about now. That wasn't my intention, but it was necessary, I felt, that I tell you these things. I've had conversations that covered this chapter with many people over the last 13 years. I have talked to coworkers and strangers that were struggling with addiction. And I didn't tell them anything different. Sugar coating and pulling punches doesn't help. It doesn't help you learn to fight the demon or give you the honest tools to even try. As I've also said before, I'm sure this isn't everything that you could face or think of. But I can only talk about things I know, things I've done and lived through. But you get the idea.

You're an addict because you made choices. Now it's time to make another choice. Perhaps the most important choice in your life. I've said a few times, and I do believe that you, like me, will always be an addict. I do not believe anyone that tells me that they "used to be an addict." I believe that an addict will always be an addict. The choice you have to make now is whether you will continue to let it control you. Will you continue to live under its spell? Will you continue your self-destructive behavior? Or will you make a different choice now? We'll talk about this again, too. But you have to answer that question. It's your life. It's your sobriety at stake. It's your choice. A choice only you can make. Because, like I said, only you can fix you.

Chapter 19: So, how do you help an addict?

That's a tough question. Because it can have so many answers, so many variables. It's not easy. Just like overcoming the demon of addiction, helping an addict and living with an addict is a challenge and struggle that can push you to, maybe even over, the edge. If you are living with someone who is an addict, I'll try to share my thoughts and advice on how to cope with them and maybe help them find a new path. Living with an addict is very, very hard. I know because I have been on this side too. I shared some of the stories of my daughter, my stepson, friends, and others. I went from being the addict to being the parent, the friend, watching someone that I cared about struggling like I had done. Making the mistakes I had made. Wishing I could do something, anything, to make them see the light that I had refused to see for so long. And feeling the pain and frustration of knowing there was nothing I could do about it.

If you're the addict, you need to read this, too. Maybe it will help you understand why everyone does what they do, why they react like they do. Why they tell you no.

The first thing, and possibly the hardest thing, to understand is the only person who can fix an addict is the addict. You can't do it. A doctor can't. Friends can't. Therapists can't. Only the addict can fix themselves. That's not saying that you, and all the others I just listed, can't help. It's just telling you an absolute truth. The addict has to fix themselves. You, other family, friends, doctors, therapists, and anyone else can only provide the tools and the instructions. You can't do the job. You can't force the job to be done. You can't do it. Only the addict can. I know this is true because I lived it. I am, as I have told you many times, an addict. I fixed myself. I didn't do it without help, without others providing the tools, the support, and the instructions when I needed it. But I had to do the work. Only I could fix me. It took me a long time to understand that. Longer still to get it right. I'm not sure my parents ever understood. They tried everything to get me to get clean, to stop using drugs. Begging, threatening, cutting me off financially. None of it worked. Until I understood and accepted that it had to be me. I had to make the choice to do it. And I had to be the one, with help as I said, to make it happen. It's hard to look at someone you care about, someone that you love, and accept that there is nothing you can do to change them. Unless they want to change themselves. It can be devastating to want so desperately to change them, to fix them, to make them sober, but be unable to make it happen. I know how it feels because I have been there with my own daughter and stepson. I knew, because I was them, that only they could do it. But it doesn't make it hurt any less. It doesn't make it any easier. And it didn't stop me from trying to make them see the light, trying to push them onto the right path, from trying to make them make better choices. I understand completely the frustration of wanting it so badly and knowing that nothing I tried made a difference. I'm telling you that I understand it isn't "just that easy" to accept that only they can fix themselves. But, easy or not, you have to accept that because it is reality. You have no choice but to accept that the addict is the only one that can make them change.

That doesn't mean that you can't help. It doesn't mean that you abandon them and let them sink or swim on their own. It just means that you have to understand some things, and that you're going to have to make some tough choices of your own. You're going to have to be strong and not give in or give up. There are things that you can do. And there are things that you can't. I have been on the receiving end of people who loved me unconditionally, that couldn't make me change or make better choices. And I've been on the side of loving people who wouldn't listen to me, wouldn't understand that I had been there, done that, and knew a way out. Maybe because I had been where they were, I was able to get to these answers faster than some. I have, as I said in the last chapter, had conversations with addicts and told them exactly what I wrote. And I've talked to people who were trying to understand addiction, trying to help an addict that they loved, and I've told them what I'm going to tell you. Again, I'm not saying that this is the only way. I'm saying that I've done it and I've seen it work. You can adapt it to your situation, can mold it to work in your circumstances, but the underlying advice and the lessons I learned through a lot of struggle and tears, are things that can help you make sense of what the addict you love is going through.

185

And how to handle some situations when they arise. Just remember, don't set your expectations too high. You have to keep your eyes wide open and understand that they might fail. They might be trying and relapse. They could be lying to you and trying to manipulate you again. Even if they are serious about getting sober, they probably won't get it right the first time they really try. You have to be their support system, their safe place. You have to tell them to try again, not to give up. You can't set the bar too high, but don't set it too low either. Be realistic. Understand that it's going to take time, and it's going to be difficult for everyone. Just don't lie to yourself, don't see things that aren't there, and always be honest with them and with yourself. And, I really hate to have to say this, you must always remember that they might never find their way to sobriety. Never give up. Never stop loving them. Even if you have to do it from a distance.

I just told you that you have to be their safe place. I want to go into that a little more, explain what I mean. You have to be a place, a person they can come to, that won't just turn your back on them, refuse to give them a chance. You can't shut them down when they are trying to talk to you and start preaching at them. You have to listen to what they are trying to say. Even if they get it mixed up, if they can't put into words what they want to, what they are feeling, and going through. You have to listen and ask questions, help them formulate the words that will give you understanding of where they are and what they are trying to say. That's not saying that you have to believe everything, or anything that they tell you. But you need to listen, without harsh judgement or reprisal so that you will have a better understanding of where they are on their path to recovery, to be able to determine if they are telling you the truth or attempting to manipulate you again. You have to listen and weigh your options based on what you are hearing from them. You can't know what is in their head unless they tell you. You can't feel what's in their heart until they show you. So be a safe place. Allow them to talk to you, to open up to you, and let you know where they really are. You don't have to give in to anything, don't have to agree with them. But they have to know that they can talk to you and that you will listen. And that you will give whatever they are asking or telling you fair consideration. If you don't agree with them, they might get mad at you. If they do, let them. Stand firm. Always. Loving them from a distance also means giving them Tough Love when that's what they need. Being a safe place doesn't mean giving in. Being their safe place means being a place of stability, a place that they can always come to and be treated with fairness, even if they don't always get what they want.

You can tell them that they have a problem. I know I said in the last chapter that the addict has to be the one to admit that they do. That doesn't mean that you can't tell them too. And you should. If you see a problem with how much they are drinking, or that they're doing drugs, being recklessly promiscuous, gambling too much, or whatever it is that has them under its spell, you should say something. That doesn't change the fact that they will have to admit it to themselves. You don't have to beat them down about it. You don't have to scream at them constantly. But you can, and should, tell them that you see a problem with their behavior. You should encourage them to really look at themselves, their situation, and that they should be honest with themselves about what they see. Just don't expect that some light bulb will suddenly come on and they'll see the error of their ways. That would be setting yourself up for more disappointment and pain. But it doesn't hurt to nudge them from time to time and encourage them to really think about it. If they start getting upset with you, getting mad, and being argumentative, back off. Let it go for a while. Don't push them too hard. Because, like I keep saying, it's ultimately their choice, their job to start their journey toward sobriety.

As addicts begin a journey toward sobriety, they will want their accomplishments to be noticed and acknowledged. This often leads to an addict making bold statements like, "I've got this," or "I'm good now" before they are ready. They will often be proud, or act like they are, of taking the first steps toward getting their lives together. And they should be proud that they have made a better choice. But that doesn't mean that they are out of the woods. You have to temper their pride and remind them that they are just getting started and that, while they should be proud that they have made a choice to try to get their lives back on track, they aren't there yet. A 30-day sobriety chip doesn't mean that they've beaten their alcoholism. A Certificate of Completion from a rehab facility doesn't mean that they'll never pick up a drug pipe or needle again. It just means that they are trying. It is a sign that they are going in the right direction, and it should be acknowledged and appreciated. But don't create a false sense of accomplishment by making more of it than it is. Don't go on social media and tell the world that your loved one is done with addiction. If they are doing that on social media, remind them that they aren't at the end of their journey and that they should probably hold off on making such sweeping pronouncements. It's acceptable to chronicle the steps they are taking and the successes they make. But they can't be allowed to go to extremes and start making statements that aren't actually true. Addicts have usually been beaten down for so long that they want to take any positive accomplishment, any good result, and show it off to the world. And many will exaggerate the accomplishment to make it sound bigger and better than it really is. They want to finally feel good about something that they are doing and show everyone who doubted them, questioned them, put them down, that they are doing better and have everything under control. Even if they really don't. They might not realize, often addicts don't realize, that they are still in a very precarious position and could easily and quickly fall back into their old routines, old habits, and their addiction. They could end up right back where they started. Or worse. So, make sure to acknowledge the good things that they are doing and the effort they have put into making progress. Just make sure that you keep your praise on pace with their journey. The road to recovery is a long one for most addicts. Trying to take shortcuts will only lead to disappointment, dead ends, and ultimate failure. Keeping them focused on where they actually are on that journey will help them make the right choices, stay focused on the finish line, and have a better chance of getting there.

They could, and most will, complain about their circumstances. They won't be happy with where they are living. They will complain that they don't have a vehicle, so it's hard for them to get to work. They might not be able to afford many luxuries, like streaming services, cable, or other entertainment, and want to whine about those things. They will often be forced to take a job making less money and with less prestige than they had before their downfall. If they start talking about these things, hinting or outright asking that you should do something to help them, provide anything, you will have to remind them that it is not your place to make anything happen. It is not your fault that they are in a place in their lives where they don't have things that they want or things that they used to have. That it wasn't you who made choices that caused them to lose any of those things. And you can't give in to them and provide any of it. You must remind them that they made choices that brought them to where they are and that they have to make other choices, better choices that will take them to where they want to be. They might tell you that without a car, getting to work is difficult if not impossible, and that because you won't help them it will be your fault if they can't keep their job. That is manipulation. That is entitlement. And it is wrong. If they can't get to work and lose their job, again, it is again because they have made a bad choice. They didn't account for everything it would take to get to that job, to do that job, or whatever the problem is. You can't allow them to bully you into providing them with transportation options. That includes driving them to and from work. Who drives you to work? You, most likely. In a vehicle that you work to pay for, that you maintain, and that you earned on your own. You don't depend on others to come and drive you around whenever you need to go to work, go to the store, or just want to go somewhere. Even if you don't own a vehicle and use public transportation, you made the choices that work for you to be able to get from where you are to where you need to be. Without having to call anyone to take you. Without having to rely on others. They can do that too. They should do it on their own. They should learn to figure out the bus schedule so they can get to work on time. They should budget for what transportation is going to cost to get them to work or anywhere else they need or want to go. If they want a car, they should work and save and buy it on their own. They might have ruined their credit on their journey to Rock Bottom and be unable to get a favorable loan. That is not your fault either. And not your place to fix. They might have to buy an older used car at a buy-here-pay-here lot. If they ask you to co-sign for them, refuse. Never financially obligate yourself to anything that you don't need and don't want to have to pay for down the road. They might get mad at you. Let them. And let them figure it out on their own. Do not allow yourself to be manipulated into further enabling them. You didn't make them make their bad choices. But you have to make them make the right ones.

Many addicts have become so accustomed to manipulating people that they have a hard time changing that approach and behavior. If they have been allowed to take advantage of you, they will expect you to continue to provide whatever you will. If they have been allowed to live a life of entitlement, they won't react well to it being taken away. But it has to be taken away. The manipulations have to stop. They can't be allowed to work anymore. Because allowing them to continue isn't helping them. It's an extension of enabling them.

Another thing that an addict might ask for is to live in your home. If you are a parent with an addict child, you might not see that as a problem. But it is. You were supposed to keep a roof over their heads when they were children, while they were growing up. You were supposed to keep them clothed and fed. That was what you signed up for when you decided to become a parent. And, whether you realized it or not, it was your job to teach them, as they were growing up, and you were doing all of those things, that is how life works when you grow up. When you become an adult, you are supposed to start taking care of yourself, managing your responsibilities, and taking care of your life. They were supposed to learn as they went to school, lived their lives, and went out into the big wide world that it was up to them where they ended up. You don't, or shouldn't, ever stop loving your child. You will always be a parent. But the dynamic changes when they become adults, too. You are still the parent. They are still the child. You can be friends, too, but that part always comes later and always comes second. You can't let yourself escape your responsibility as a parent to be a friend. If you do, you are not doing your child any favors. Being their friend might be easier than being their parent. It might be more "fun" to hang out than to enforce rules and boundaries. But you have an absolute obligation to be a parent first. Always first. That applies to other aspects of life, and dealing with an addict, and we will probably come back to it more than once before we reach our journey's end.

Allowing your addict child to move back into your home can cause many problems. If they expect to move back into your home, their childhood home, without paying rent, that shouldn't be allowed. If you allow that to happen, you relieve them of a responsibility that should be theirs and theirs alone. Providing shelter. When the time comes for them to seek their own place again in the future, they might not be prepared to pay their rent, their utilities, meet all of their financial obligations. If they are allowed to live without having to bear the responsibility of paying for these things, they could become used to spending their money on other things and will be unable to, and probably resentful of having to, give up their wants to satisfy their needs and necessities. This could lead to them asking to borrow money, or expecting money to be provided, which could lead to arguments, hurt feelings, or even their return to their addiction and substance abuse.

And it's not only the financial issues of allowing an adult child to return to your home. They aren't children anymore. When they were growing up, you probably set a curfew, had rules, and expected that your expectations be respected. If they are now adults, they might not accept that there will be a curfew, that there are still rules. That it is still YOUR HOME. They might think, might even say out loud, that they are adults and can come and go as they please, that they can do whatever they want because they aren't children. They won't respect that it is YOUR HOME and that you and your rules should be, must be, respected. If you have to get up early to go to work, you can't have them coming and going at all hours, interrupting your rest. They might feel that since they are adults, that you can't tell them it's unacceptable to come in at midnight. They might not respect that you have to get up for work at 5 am and don't need to be woken up at random times.

They could want to spend time with their friends and invite them into your home without considering your feelings or asking if it would be acceptable. Again, it is your home and not a community hang out. They might get mad and tell you that you are trying to keep them from having friends, a social life, and that you are being selfish and unreasonable. All the while refusing to recognize that it is YOUR HOME and that YOU make the rules.

These are just a couple of examples. They could have no hesitation in emptying your refrigerator and never contribute to the grocery bill. They could leave all the lights on in the house and never help pay the electric bill. They could order pay-per-view content on your cable or streaming platforms and let you pay for it. In other words, they could take advantage of you, use you, in countless ways that are unfair and disrespectful to you, and never give it a second thought. So, in my opinion, it is not a good idea to allow an adult addict child to move back into your home. They should seek shelter somewhere else. Either get their own house or apartment, whatever they can afford, even if it is "below their standards." Even live in a shelter while they work and save money to be able to afford rent for a place of their own. Just because they don't want to live in a place that they find unacceptable, or a shelter, doesn't mean that you have to provide them with a place to live. You have to provide YOU a place to live. You have to make sure you have your bills paid, you have food, that you can meet all of your responsibilities. They created their own situation. Let them figure out a way out of it. Again, they aren't entitled to a home. They have to earn it. And it doesn't have to be YOURS.

The same thing applies to vehicles. Don't let them "borrow" yours. If you allow them to use your vehicle, you could end up being without it when you need it. If they drive your car to work, you won't have access to it until their workday is finished and they return. What are you supposed to do if you have an appointment, need to go to the store, or have to go to work yourself? It's your car, not theirs. You shouldn't be inconvenienced just because they don't want to be. You didn't make choices that led to you losing your car, or your home. You didn't squander everything on beer, drugs, or something else. You made responsible choices, honored your obligations, paid your bills, and earned what you have. It is yours. And it should be there for you to use when you need to or want to. And what do you do if your adult addict child is driving your vehicle under the influence and gets pulled over and arrested? Your car would probably be towed, leaving you with a bill for that, not counting the charge for impounding the vehicle. They could also wreck your car, total it, and leave you without it. What would you do then? They obviously couldn't afford a vehicle of their own, that's why they were borrowing yours. So, you know that they won't be buying you another car. If they did wreck your vehicle, you could face legal consequences for allowing them to drive it.

Especially if they hit another car and injured someone. You could be taken to court and made to pay damages. You could end up losing your home and everything you own. You shouldn't have to suffer because of their mistakes. So, don't. Let them figure it out for themselves. And that means being their own personal taxi. Don't drive them everywhere they want to go. Especially if they aren't pitching in on gas, maintenance, insurance. You should see a pattern starting to emerge here. They are responsible for their circumstances, and it's not your place to fix their mistakes.

I'm not saying that you should never do anything with them. I'm saying that it should be on your terms. Always on your terms. If you have a free day, and they are free too, you are well within your rights to go pick them up, take them to lunch, or just spend the day together. In fact, you should spend time with them if they are on a better path, making better choices, and working their way back up. It will help them by showing them that you are still there, still engaged, still care about them, and still want them to stay the course they are on. But it shouldn't be because they demand it or ask for other reasons. It should be because you want to. And because you want to spend time with them, not enable them or allow them to manipulate you. If you are in the neighborhood and they need a ride to work, offer to drive them. Just don't let it become an expectation or entitlement. And don't "find yourself in the neighborhood" every day. Don't pretend that you're doing it because you want to, but are really doing it because you feel sorry for them or some other reason. Make sure you do anything that you do on your terms and for good reasons. If you do go and spend time with them and they start asking you to do it more often, and "remembering" that they had somewhere they need to go, for example, you should say no. You should remind them that you aren't their personal taxi service and that you won't allow them to treat you that way. If they try to demand that you do something, you should flat out refuse. If they demand that you come and drive them to work, the store, anywhere, you should tell them that you will not do it. Period. When they want a reason, they don't get one. They don't deserve it. Your answer is no, and that is all that they need to know. If they start to get pushy, rude, or start making accusations, end the conversation. Don't engage. Don't argue. Don't explain. End the conversation. When they want to know why you hung up on them, let them know that you will not participate in a conversation if you aren't treated with

200

respect. That you won't be accused of something that isn't fair or accurate, like the fact that they don't have a car but don't want to walk, and that you will end every communication that goes in that direction. Don't make exceptions and don't give in to their tantrums or demands. That's part of what led to where they are now. Reinforce that they have to be independent, that they have to figure things out for themselves. Remind them that you didn't put them where they are, that they did. And it's their responsibility to find the solutions that they need.

Don't give them money. This is apparently something that comes up very often when dealing with an addict. I have read posts on social media, read books about this, seen movies where it happened, about addicts asking for money, for more and more, until the people who were trying to help lost everything. They gave and gave, the addict took and took, until there was nothing left. They will come to you will all sorts of stories about how they had a situation that caused them to be short on the rent, or a car payment, the electric bill, or something else. It will always be someone or something else's fault. It will have been out of their control. But they need help, or they are going to lose something, their family is going to suffer, or whatever the case may be. Many of us are guilty of giving in and giving them what they asked for. Maybe we insisted that it be repaid, and it might have been in the beginning. We might have gotten into the habit of just giving it to them without pushing for more information, without finding the truth behind the repeated "need." And at some point, they probably stopped repaying us. And we still felt pity, sympathy for them, and kept giving in to them anyway. It might have been because we felt sorry for their children, our grandchildren, in many cases. It might have been that we didn't want to hear their whining and complaining, and it was just easier to pay their car payment than hear the crying and excuses. Whatever the reason we did it, we were enabling them. We should have started asking tough questions at the beginning. We should have asked the person that we knew was an alcoholic if they had had the money for their alcohol. We should have asked the drug addict if they had gotten their fix. The gambler, if he had been at the casino. But we didn't. Why didn't we? Because we didn't want to hurt their feelings? We didn't want to argue with them? We didn't want to hear the lies and excuses? Or because we didn't want to stand up to them, to tell them that we knew that they had blown the house payment drinking with their friends and partying. Because we didn't want to say that your dope was more important than making your car payment. That feeding that slot machine was more important than feeding your family. Because we didn't want to call them out. Because the truth is that if they had the money to afford to feed their addiction, they had the money to pay their bills. That is just the truth. If an alcoholic had the money to buy their beer, they had the money to pay the rent. If the drug addict had the money to pay for their pills or meth, or heroin, they could have made the car payment. If the gambler had the money to keep spinning the roulette wheel, they had the money to pay the electric bill. But they chose to spend that money on their addiction. And we chose to replace it. The truth, the reality, is that we bought that beer, that drug, placed that bet. It's just simple substitution. We gave the money that was spent on those things to spend on what it should have been spent on. We could have just as easily gone to the package store, or whatever description fits, for them and bought their substance of choice for them. Because replacing what money they are throwing away is doing that. And it's not just giving them the actual cash. Buying them groceries, paying the electric bill, making the car payment, whatever it is, is the same thing. It's making the money they need to satisfy their addiction available because what the money was supposed to be used for will still be paid. This can apply to non-addicts, too. But it certainly applies to addicts, and it's how we unwittingly feed their addiction even though we would never consciously do that. So, stop giving them money. No matter what their reason, no matter what their excuse, no matter how much they beg. If they are able to satisfy their addiction, they are able to pay for their own lives.

I've been addressing moving back into your home, using your vehicles, being part of your life again, asking for financial help, without specifying whether or not the addict is still under the influence of their substance or trying to get sober. My answers don't change. I stand by everything I have said. That it's a bad idea, and I personally wouldn't allow any of it. I haven't and I won't. If the addict in question is still actively in their addiction, still doing the things that have ruined their lives and put them in their predicament, what do you think will happen if you allow them to come back into your home? To drive your vehicle? If you start, or continue paying their bills? Nothing will change except that everything will get worse. If you give them a place to live, feed them, provide them with a vehicle or transportation, what incentive will they have to try to change things for themselves? What reason would they have to stop their substance abuse, get sober, and start taking care of themselves? What will likely happen is that your life will suffer and possibly be destroyed right along with theirs. If you give them money, what happens when your car breaks down? Or your air conditioning unit stops working? Or the water heater isn't heating water anymore? You see a pattern here again, I hope. You can't allow an addict to keep taking from you. It doesn't matter if you "have it to give" or not. You shouldn't do it. If they are determined to hit Rock Bottom, get out of their way. Don't try to slow them down. They'll just push you in front and use you to cushion the crash. And they won't care.

If they aren't getting what they want, they could steal from you. That can't be allowed. Ever. Period. End of conversation. If an addict is willing to steal, they, in my opinion, are willing to suffer the consequences. Whatever they are. If they steal money or your belongings, call the police. If they throw a tantrum and destroy your property, press charges. If they threaten you, or worse, put their hands on you, have them arrested. You might not want to think that someone you care about, your child or friend, or whoever, would do any of these things. But they could. It could be that it's already happened, some of the things that I laid out, or all of them, and you didn't do anything about it. It could be that they've done countless other things that I haven't talked about or personally encountered, and you just let it go. Because you care about them. Because you don't want to see them hurt, see them go to jail, suffer, or face negative consequences. But let me ask you a question. If they did any of those things – stole from you, destroyed something that belonged to you, physically threatened or attacked you – did they care about you? Did they stop and consider what they were doing and the damage it could cause to you? No. They didn't think, and they didn't care. Why? Because they cared more about getting what they wanted, satisfying their addiction, than they did about themselves or you. They might not have done any of those things if they weren't under the influence, under the spell of a demon substance. But they did. And they should suffer the consequences, no matter what they are. And that wouldn't be your fault either. It, like their addiction, would be because of their own choices.

Don't feed their self-pity either. Don't allow them to portray themselves as the victim. Don't listen to any of it. When they start making excuses and blaming everyone and everything else, and they will, you can't even pretend that you agree. You have to see things for what they are. You have to have your eyes wide open and see reality. You can't let them spin a web of deceit and lies and allow yourself to get caught up and carried away. When they start rewriting the truth to fit their situation, to shift the blame away from themselves, to always being the one under attack, you have to be able to see through the smoke and find the truth. Even when they refuse to admit the truth, you have to find it and you have to hold on to it. You can't allow them to get away with blaming their employer for putting a target on them when they laid out of work because they were too hung over to go. You can't allow the addict to say that their spouse left them, make unsubstantiated accusations about infidelity or anything else, when it was their substance, and possibly emotional and physical abuse that pushed them out the door. You can't let them convince you that their car got wrecked because a cat ran out into the road when you know that they were driving under the influence. You can't ever participate in their lies. You can't ever allow them to play victim when they are the guilty one. You might feel sorry for them, that is human nature. But you can't allow them to pull you into their pity-party and feed their attempts to escape responsibility. If you allow them to think that their deceptions are being believed, you are only encouraging them to embellish more, to tell bigger, more outrageous lies, and to run faster and further to evade the ultimate conclusion – accountability.

You have to hold an addict accountable. If you don't, you aren't helping them, you aren't doing them a favor. You are encouraging more of the same bad behavior. You are leading them to believe that they are being successful in hiding their problems, which will only lead to the situation deteriorating even more. You are encouraging more manipulation and giving them an invitation to try to fool you, use you, and hurt you even more. If they are under the influence of their addiction, they won't want to hear it, they will argue, and it could get ugly, but you have to do it. You can't let them get away with things that aren't right, aren't good for anyone, and that only lead to worse situations. You can't make them change, you can't make them make better choices, you can't make them get sober. But you have to hold them accountable. No matter the result. If they steal, they should go to jail and pay the price. If they won't respect your home and your rules, they should be made to leave. If they attack you, physically, verbally, or any other way, they should be arrested and suffer the consequences, no matter how severe.

Don't just automatically believe them when they say they've seen the light either. Just because they go to rehab, start going to meetings or to church, or are doing things that give the appearance of trying to get on the right path doesn't mean it's true. It doesn't mean they're sincere. Many addicts will do these things to try to manipulate you into thinking that they want to get better so that you'll be more open and willing to "help" them. You can't fall for it. We have all probably been fooled by someone who's done this. If we continue to be, then we have to stop. We have to see things for what they really are. We have to see the truth. No matter if it hurts, or if it's what we've wanted so badly to see. That doesn't mean that if an addict tells us that they are going into rehab because they know they have a problem that we should call them liars. We should tell them that their choice is the right one, and that we hope that it works. And that we will be waiting and watching to see the outcome. We don't have to offer anything more than that. Nothing more than the chance to show us that they are sincere. We don't owe them money, shelter, or anything else. It might be hard not to want to do more for them, but we can't. We have to let them prove themselves. No matter what they ultimately prove. If they are attempting to fool us, manipulate, then they will eventually get tired of keeping up the charade, and the truth will show itself. They will leave the facility, hospital, or wherever they went, and return to their old ways. The alcoholism, drug use, whatever their method of self-destruction, will resume, and their lie will be exposed for what it was. If they are sincere, they will complete whatever program they entered, they will have taken full advantage of positive opportunities to find help and learn better life skills, and they will be sober and ready to rebuild their lives. We will be there to see it. Because we were willing to give them a chance to show us.

Also, don't feel guilty because you are unwilling to fall for their manipulations, their lies, their games. That you refuse to give them any more money, let them use you for a place to stay, transportation. That you won't believe the lies and refuse to play the games any longer. You don't owe them any of that. You gave them what you could, what you should have as a parent or friend. You didn't choose to throw that away and destroy the relationship. They did. So, you shouldn't feel guilty because they are in the shape they are in. You didn't make them make the choice to start the self-destructive behavior. You didn't make them become addicted to something. They made those choices. Without consulting you. Against your wishes and advice. No, we don't want to see someone we care about lose everything, see their family fall apart, see their lives devastated. We can't imagine how it feels to be homeless. But don't feel guilty when you say no, enough is enough. Don't feel guilty when you tell them that it was their own choices that caused everything that happened to them. Don't let them cause you to question yourself, to doubt that you are doing the right thing by refusing to be used, manipulated, and hurt, and that you are right for not enabling them any longer. Don't let it lead you to depression. You will worry about them. You will still care about them. But you can't, and should not, help them anymore. You have to recognize that they need more help than you are able to give, and that they need HELP, not enabling. When they keep coming back and asking for more, demanding more, trying to play on your pity and sympathy, don't feel guilty for saying "NO."

You have a responsibility to yourself first. You have to make sure that your health, your sanity, your life are your first priority. You can't let yourself go, can't ignore yourself, your health, to try to fix them. I know a woman who sat by her son in the hospital, wondering if he was going to pull through again or if this was the time that he didn't make it, while she was suffering from major health problems and was days, maybe less, away from death herself. She ignored symptoms and signs in herself that should have made her run to the hospital because she refused to leave his side. She finally couldn't ignore it any longer and did go to the hospital. The doctors did a test, a procedure, and rushed her into the hospital and emergency surgery. She had a condition that could have taken her life, that was, by the doctor's account, very close to ending her life. His question during the procedure that found the problem was, "How is she still alive?" He wasn't asking to exaggerate. He was seriously asking because he was surprised that it hadn't killed her already. She hadn't been looking out for herself. She had allowed herself to be consumed by her addict son's problem, and it almost cost her everything. And where would he have been if she had died? Who would he have had then? She was the only parent he had left, as his father had died a few years earlier. His wife had already left him because of his alcoholism. His son was a child and unable to do anything. He had a brother, but he didn't live close, had a demanding job, and a family of his own to take care of. So, if she had continued to ignore her symptoms, and had ultimately lost her life, who would have taken care of him? We're all lucky that we don't have to know how that would have played out.

She was rendered unable to care for him for a while after her surgery. But eventually they both healed and were able to resume their lives. She learned something from it. She learned that her self-care had to start coming first. Physical health, but also emotional and mental health too. She had allowed herself to become so wrapped up in his alcoholism that it affected every part of her life. She wasn't completely ignoring the rest of her life, but she was partially checked out on everything and everyone else. It took some time. And therapy. But she came to see that his addiction, his storm, wasn't her storm. That his burden wasn't for her to bear. She never stopped loving her son, but she had to learn to step back and love him from a distance. I got that line from her. Love from a distance. It resonated and it stuck with me. Because it's what we have to do. We have to love tough, and we have to love from where we are safe ourselves, from a distance.

It's also important when talking to an addict that you be very straight forward, very honest, and very firm. Don't use ambiguous language, don't leave questions hanging and unanswered. Be direct and always be truthful. Don't try to lead an addict to a conclusion, don't try to let them figure out what you mean. Just say what you mean. Completely, clearly. Don't leave room for doubt, don't let them think that there is a weakness that they can exploit. Make sure that they know that you mean what you say and always stick to what you said. Stand firm. Do not allow yourself to be drawn into endless, circular arguments that don't lead to anything. Don't let them shout you down when you point out that they are being irresponsible or unreasonable. Don't attack them unnecessarily, but if they start, don't retreat. Stand your ground always. Be fair, don't make unrealistic requests, or demand the impossible. But if they ask for something, if it's not something that you are able or willing to give, tell them no. Don't hesitate, don't beat around the bush hoping the request will just go away. If the answer is no, then say it. Say "No." They don't have to like it. But don't give them a choice. Don't allow them to change your mind. You have to stand up for yourself, or you'll find yourself caught up in their storm, and that's a place you don't want or need to be. If they get mad at you and refuse to talk to you because they didn't get their way, wait them out. Don't chase them down, don't beg them to talk to you. And never give in to them so they will stop being upset. Appeasement never works. It only makes things worse because the one being appeased sees weakness, and the one giving in starts finding it easier to let them win. And giving them what they want won't help. It only delays the inevitable. They're determined to find Rock Bottom. The longer you allow them to search for it, the harder they will crash into it when they find it.

Saying "No" doesn't make you the bad guy. It might be hard to understand, for both of you, but it's the best thing you can say to an addict.

When the addict finally gets to their Rock Bottom, it probably won't be a pretty sight. Few, if any, people who hit rock bottom escape without injury. No matter how you try, you can't stop them. Like I said, they'll either push you in front to cushion the crash or, at the very least, grab on and drag you down with them. You have no choice but to let them find it and hit it on their own. And you can't automatically pick up the pieces either. You will want to. You will want to stop them before they crash. But you can't. If you do, you'll just be putting off what's coming. I told my dad that if he'd offered help when I hit rock bottom, I'd have asked for a pick and shovel to keep digging. Most addicts are like that. You have to let it happen. They have to feel the impact to realize that they have to make different choices. If you interrupt, if you get in the way, you only lose part of you and delay what is still coming. If you are in the way and get pulled into the crash, you won't be able to help them when they do really want to climb out. No matter how hard it is, no matter how it hurts to watch, you have to leave them to their choices and consequences. You didn't make them start. You can't make them stop. All you can do is watch it happen. Hopefully, they'll just get banged up and learn from it. Hopefully, they will want something different and will see that they have to start making different, better choices if they want things to change. Hopefully, they will admit, finally, that they have a problem and that only they can fix it.

Never beg or plead with an addict to stop. Don't try to bribe them or cajole them. Don't waste your time threatening them or telling them how their actions, choices, and behaviors are ruining their lives. Or yours. They know, deep down inside, whether they are willing to admit it or not. None of these things are likely to make a difference. If they are actively in their addiction, they won't hear what you're trying to get them to understand, or they simply won't care. You can tell them how it's affecting you, your mental state, your health, but they probably still won't listen or change anything. It won't be because they don't care, that they don't love you. It will be because they are under the addiction demon's spell and aren't in control anymore. They have handed the reins over to addiction and are being driven and controlled by something that neither of you understand. Begging, threatening, any of those things can lead to disagreements and arguments, more hurt feelings, and damage to the already broken relationship. So don't waste your time trying to use this approach to get them to change. It will only lead to more frustration, more anxiety, and more distance between you. You can let them know, but don't keep beating a dead horse and repeating it every time you talk to them. Again, you have to remember, and they do too, that only they can make things different. Only they can make different choices. Only they can fix themselves.

Some will never understand that. Some will never see the error of their choices and will never return to a clean, sober life. Some will be lost before their time. It is a sad truth that not everyone can be saved. I, like I'm sure all of you, wish that it were different. We never want to see a life end through needless, careless means. We never want someone to lose their life because they made bad choices. But it does happen. It happened to my former co-worker. He's not the only one. It happens thousands of times every year. It doesn't have to happen. It can be avoided. But only the addict can make that happen. As I have said again and again, only the addict can fix themselves.

Hopefully, they will. Maybe they will realize that they have to change and start taking the initiative, making the choices to fix their lives and themselves. When they do, if they are sincere and really want to get things right, you will still be their safe place. If they prove to you that they are serious, that they want to make better choices, to be sober and have a better life, then support them. You don't have to support them financially. You don't have to do everything for them. But emotionally, mentally, you can. Go back to where I talked about pride. Be proud of them as they start their journey to sobriety, acknowledge every milestone that they reach. Celebrate every success. Just remember to do it all in proportion to where they are on the journey, what milestone they have reached, what they have achieved. Getting sober takes time. Sometimes it takes a long time. But it is possible. I am proof that it is. Don't give up on an addict. Don't let them pull you down with them, but don't hold them down if they truly want to climb back up. If they are successful, they will have to learn to live their lives all over again. They will have many hurdles, many challenges. Let them know that they aren't alone anymore, that they have your support. That you believe in them. Keep watching them, keep making sure they are not slipping. Like Ronald Reagan said many years ago, "Trust but verify."

If they make it to the other side, the side where they are clean and sober, not engaging in self-destructive behaviors, and are working on rebuilding their lives, they will have some things to do to finish the job. I'll come back to some of these later, and expand on this part, too, but I will discuss one thing now that I believe is a part of a successful journey.

I said in my conversation to the addict that they owe an apology to everyone that they hurt while on their explorations of addiction. And I meant it. They probably won't remember everything, specific details, and won't be able to lay them all out. We might remember every single one of them. If they ask for the specifics, the details, then be completely honest. Tell it all. If they don't ask, but you feel it's necessary that it all be on the table, tell them anyway. If they get mad, if they won't hear it, then don't continue the conversation. You didn't ask them to betray you, to hurt you. If they are coming to you to apologize, they should know what they are apologizing for. All of it. If they are sincere, they will hear you out, they will want to know so that they fully understand what they are apologizing for. I told you that when I had this conversation with my daughters, I asked them to tell me things that I didn't remember, or that I hadn't even realized I had done. And that it felt like I was a punching bag because I had done a lot. I really didn't want to hear all of the things I had done, did not enjoy being reminded of how badly I had screwed things up, but I had to know. I had to fully comprehend the depths of the pain I had caused. They didn't tell me because they wanted to hurt me. They told me because if I didn't acknowledge what I had done that my apology would have been less real, less sincere. I didn't get mad at either of them for their honesty. I took my blows and let them say what they needed to say. If they chose to leave things out, to exclude things I had done that hurt them, that was on them. When they were finished, I told them that I knew that the words weren't enough, that nothing could ever take any of it back, but that I truly regretted everything I had done to hurt them, to hurt myself, and to have brought the devastation I did down on our lives. I promised them that I would never allow myself to become that person again, and that I would always try to make myself and my life better. I'm going to come back to this later, but for now, what I'm about to say is important and will tie into that later.

If they do come to you, if you do have that conversation with them after they have gotten clean and sober, gotten their lives together, you have a choice to make. Do you accept their apology? Either way, that is the moment that you have to decide. You can't drag it out. You can't hold it over their head and use it to manipulate them. You can't use it to browbeat them into doing something or behaving a certain way. You either accept the apology, or you don't. If you don't, then say so and move on with your life. Don't try to come back later and exact another ounce of flesh. You have the right not to accept it. You must decide if you can or if you can't. It doesn't make you a bad person, an evil person, to not be able to accept their apology. Only you know how badly it hurt, how deeply it cut, or how or if the wounds have healed. But you can't hold it over them, you can't expect them to keep begging. They have been through a lot. They don't deserve to be beaten down anymore. They deserve a straight answer, no matter what it is. If you do accept their apology, then accept it fully and move on. It doesn't mean that those things never happened. It doesn't mean that you won't be somewhat guarded for a while, maybe forever. But you can't expect them to be constantly repeating the apology either. If you do accept it, you are telling them that you are giving them a chance to show you that things are going to be different, that they won't hurt or betray you again. If they do, cut them loose and move on. Don't look back. But if they keep their word, allow them to be who they are becoming, don't continue to see the old them, the using addict. Let them be sober and clean and see them for who they are now. Anything less is unfair to everyone.

I could go on and on giving you examples of things you can encounter when coping with an addict. I have given you examples of things that I have either done myself or been on the other side of. I know that there are an infinite number of possibilities and that nothing is impossible when living through addiction or trying to help someone who is. Just remember to always keep your eyes open, always trust your instincts, and never forget that everything could fall apart again in an instant. If you are trying to help an addict find their way back to themselves, always remain on guard. Don't be too harsh, don't be cruel. Be firm, be strong, and never yield. Be fair. And also, never forget that everything you do, everything you want for them, everything you try could end up being unappreciated, unrecognized, and in vain. Don't tell them that they are going to fail. Tell them that they can do it, that they can find sobriety and themselves again. Don't take their hope away, but don't let yourself get lost in false hope either. Always remember to see things for what they are, see the truth. It would be my wish that never again would anyone lose their battle and their life to addiction, to substance abuse. But some will. Some will be lost without anyone seeing it coming. Others right in front of us, even though we were trying everything that we could to help them, to get them to change. And some will be fighting, trying, but won't have enough fight left to make it out of the battle. But if we are vigilant, hopefully we can catch them early, before they are so lost that we can't find them and bring them back. If we keep ourselves focused, take care of our health, mental and physical, and allow God to help us help them, maybe we can save them. They can't do it alone. And if you can't, you can talk to someone, too. You can talk to a therapist or other medical professional. They could give you different perspectives, new ways to approach the addict, and help you make sure you are in a good place while you're trying to help them. Remember, if you're not in a good place, if you're not the best you that you can be, how good will you be for the addict that you love, that you're trying to save?

223

Chapter 20: The guilt and the fear

I have talked to many people over the last few years, some very close to me and some strangers. I have read and been told about things that were posted on social media platforms by parents who were trying to understand their addicted child, trying to help them, trying to get them to change their lives. I have felt these feelings myself as I dealt with my daughter's addiction and stepson's alcoholism. I have seen my wife suffer with it. The guilt that we feel when we tell the addict that we love "No." And the fear of what comes next, the unknown future that is waiting for us.

It is natural to want to help someone that we love. Especially our children. When they are growing up, we don't want to see them get hurt, be afraid, or have to do without something that they need. When they are young, it is our responsibility to make sure that their needs are met. It is our job to comfort them, to reassure them when they are frightened. To wipe the tears away and get the band-aids when they get injured. It's just what parents do. The instinct to continue doing those things never fully goes away. When they are grown, we usually don't have to do those things anymore. Hopefully, we have taught them to see things as adults, with maturity, so that they aren't scared of the monster under the bed, they are responsible, work, and are able to meet their responsibilities and have everything that they need. And, hopefully, they aren't routinely getting scraped knees and elbows anymore. But when they fall into the clutches of addiction, they often revert to their childish ways and don't do those things. Some still get part of it right, some don't get it at all. And they very often expect someone to take care of everything and provide those things for them. And the first place they normally go is back to their parents.

It is painful to be the parent when this happens. To see the child that you raised under the control of something that you, and probably they, don't understand is very frustrating and causes a lot of stress and fear. Especially if you raised them to know better. As I told you before, I didn't understand what I was putting my parents through until I found myself watching my daughter living in her addiction. I couldn't have comprehended the level of hell that I put them through, wouldn't have believed it if they had told me. So, your child, the addict that you love, won't realize that they're doing it to you either. I would hope that they aren't doing it intentionally, even though they are trying to manipulate you, to get you to enable even more bad choices and behavior. No matter the reason that they are doing it, the pain, the fear, and the frustration are all very real, and they never seem to go away.

But you shouldn't feel guilty for telling your child "No." You should, as I said in the last chapter, set rules and boundaries and stick to them. No matter what excuses they make, no matter what stories they tell, and no matter how pitifully they cry and beg. Or threaten. I was very clear and very serious about how any threat, whether physical or verbal, be handled. You will be tempted, as many are, as I was, to give in and give them whatever it is that they are asking for. You will feel sorry for them if they are losing their home, their car, or their belongings. You will want to stop those things from happening and the pain and damage that it will cause. But it's not your responsibility. It's not your fault that they are facing these things, and it's not your place to pay for them. So do not allow your feelings of compassion for them, your feelings of guilt for not giving in to them, to make you bend and further enable them. If you have been doing that, stop. Explain to them that you can't keep giving them everything that you have, that you need, to maintain your home and your life. You can tell them, as I told my daughter and stepson, that it is not fair to ask that you work, that you do the things that you are supposed to do, and then pay for their mistakes with any money that you have left. It's not fair to expect, or ask, that you pay their rent, their car payments, buy their groceries, or anything else. If you do pay for things for them, it will become a habit that neither of you will be able to easily break. So, do not get into the habit of paying for their lives. I know that I am repeating this, but I am doing it for a reason. So that maybe you will see that I am serious about it, and that you should not be giving them money. Giving them money, as I also said in the last chapter, isn't paying their bills. It's paying for their addiction. You might not see it that way, you might disagree completely, but I assure you that I am correct. I know because when I was the addict, anyone that gave me any amount of money only allowed me to have that much of any money I already had to be used to buy

227

my drugs. I know because I saw it happen with my daughter and my stepson. And I felt guilty when I started telling them "No," too. I didn't like seeing them struggle, to see them lose things. I didn't want to see them lose a car, lose an apartment, face living on the street. But I knew that I couldn't afford to pay my bills, meet my obligations, and pay theirs too. Especially when they always seemed to have money for drugs or alcohol. So, I stopped doing it. I said, "No." You have to do that, too. You have to draw the line and not allow it to be crossed. You aren't "helping" them, you are only prolonging the inevitable. You aren't stopping their march toward the cliff. You're only adding a few steps before they reach the edge. If you allow it to go on for too long, you might be pulled over the edge with them. I have heard and read stories about people who kept giving and giving until they lost their homes, until they faced living on the streets, when they had done nothing to cause it. Other than having too much compassion. Other than giving in too many times. You will almost certainly feel guilty when you stop enabling them. But you must stand firm, you must stop enabling them and let them face the consequences that their choices have created.

Many people have told me that they continue to give in, to provide money or other assistance to their addicted children, because they fear what could happen if they stop. They have many fears. Some are afraid that their child will get angry and pull away, will stop communicating with them. That they won't know where their child is, what condition they are in, if they are alive or dead. They say that their biggest fear is that one day they will receive a call, or a knock at their door, and it will be someone telling them that their child has lost their life. They have said that they couldn't bear the guilt, the feeling of responsibility, if that were to happen. So that fear compels them to continue giving in, even when they know that they shouldn't. I have felt that same fear. I told you about my daughter and I having a serious fight and falling-out. That we didn't speak for close to one year. I'm not exaggerating. I didn't know where she was, where she was staying, if she was working, if she was hungry. If she was even alive. I did feel some guilt that our situation had risen to that level. I did fear that something would happen and that I would have lost her forever, that I would never have the chance to talk to her again. That I would never see her again. My wife has told me many times that she has had these fears for her son, my stepson. I have had the same

229

fears for him, too. But we had to stop enabling them. We had to stop allowing their situations to cause a reaction. We had to stop allowing the guilt we felt for wanting to stop enabling them to weaken our resolve. We had to stop enabling them. If we didn't, we were only going to allow them to continue to destroy themselves and probably destroy ourselves at the same time.

We did stop. We did say "No." We had no choice but to for our own sakes, for our own sanity. We had to stop allowing the feelings of fear and guilt to drive our choices and start making choices that were in our best interest and were, honestly, in theirs too. We had to leave them to the consequences of their choices and actions and let them figure out how to change their lives. My daughter figured it out first. I told you about that, her crashing into her Rock Bottom and the choices she made to turn her life around. My stepson has had a harder time finding his way, but is making progress and starting to make better choices. My daughter didn't get it right the first time she tried. He didn't either. But they both kept trying and didn't give in to despair and just lay down. They kept fighting, and they still fight for that better life every day.

I told you that my daughter overdosed three times, that I know of, and had to be saved by medical intervention. If it wasn't for Narcan and fast response times, she wouldn't be alive today. She wouldn't have ever had the opportunity to make the better choices that have her on the way to a happy, successful life. My stepson, as I also told you, has been hospitalized multiple times, some of them he was reaching for the darkness of the other side, but was pulled back by God's grace and the doctors who delivered it. I remind you of these things to show you that those fears are very real and that they are justified.

The worst can happen. The addict that you love, that you so desperately want to see get their lives turned around and together, can fail in the worst way and lose their life. But that can happen whether you are talking to them, seeing them, or not. The fear that you could lose them is not irrational. It is very real, and the reality is that it is very possible. But you still can't let that fear make you give in to what you know isn't best for them. Or for you. You can't allow your feelings of guilt, your fears, to push you into continued enabling, because if you continue, you could be bringing that end even faster.

It's difficult to juggle all the emotions and situations that living with an addict presents. You might need to seek help, therapy, or whatever help you need, to be able to make sense of it and to keep your sanity. If you do, then do it. There is no shame in asking for help. For an addict or for someone who is trying to love and help an addict. But you must do whatever it takes to stop yourself from getting lost in your guilt and fear. You must, as I also said in the last chapter, always take care of you first. If you're not in a good place yourself, you won't be in a place where you can help them the right way when they really need it.

Chapter 21: Now, the rest of my story

I've shared a lot of things with you, but there is more that you need to know. Some of the things I've told you are things that I never told anyone before. Not even my dad, my wife, or my closest friend. I'm telling you all of it now because I promised that I would be completely honest, and to show you that just because you walk through Hell doesn't mean that you have to stay there. I had someone tell me recently, and many times throughout my life, that everyone has skeletons in their closet. I'm opening that door and bringing mine out to show you. Again, not because I'm proud of them. But to fully understand what I'm trying to tell you, to fully grasp the seriousness of everything, you need to know the whole story.

I have left out a lot. Because it doesn't matter, it doesn't have anything to do with my addiction. It's not relevant and would just muddy the waters. It doesn't matter where I went to High School, what kind of car I have, or where I work. So, I left that part out.

While I have told you a lot, there is still more that you need to know. I'm going to go back to the beginning again. Not to repeat what I've already told you, but because there are some things that I didn't tell you then because they didn't directly matter to what we were discussing at the time. These were other things that stood apart, and alone, but that I think you need to know to fully appreciate where I was and how I got here.

I did have a wonderful childhood. Growing up on a farm taught me many things. How to feed and milk cows. How to work with and ride horses. I rode dirt bikes and go-carts, loved swimming in the summer, camping, and all of the things that come with growing up in the country. My parents were very much engaged in my life. They encouraged me to be serious about school and my education. They took me to church almost every Sunday. They taught me right from wrong. I never saw my dad touch alcohol. I only saw my mother drink wine after I turned 19. And then only a couple of times. Neither of them ever did drugs, never got arrested, never did anything they weren't supposed to do. They raised me that way, and they made sure that the words they said were backed up by their actions. They taught me by example.

As you already know, I started growing up and thought that I was ready for life, and that I was wrong. I won't go into that again. I only say that again to once again say that I didn't learn any of my bad behaviors, or learn to make my bad choices, from watching them. I knew better, I should have behaved better. I shouldn't have broken their hearts. But I did.

And, like I have told you, I didn't follow their example when I was raising my daughters. My daughters had to see me drinking alcohol, smoking marijuana, doing harder drugs. My parents had never done any of that, but I still ended up doing what I did. My girls did see all of that, and they ended up emulating my behavior. Whether they would have done what they did had I been the example a good father should have been, we will never know. We never had the chance to find out.

I know now, after many years of looking back at everything that I have done and lived through and conversations with them, that I hurt them in many more ways than just marrying my second wife. I was doing things that hurt them before she came into the picture. And I didn't stop after she was pushed out of it. I would never have admitted it then, but I was not a good father. I didn't beat them or anything like that, but there are many more things than that that make a parent good or bad. I was absent as a father. It wasn't always the case, but as they got older, it was. More often than not. And that was when they needed me to be there most.

I told you about the conversation I had with them when I asked them to tell me everything that I had done to hurt them, and the things that I knew that I had done. I had told them that I was sorry before that night. But I had never been fully aware of just how much hurt I had caused and had never been completely sincere about it. Many times, I would say it when I was still using drugs, and I would say it just to relieve myself of the guilt I felt, knowing that what I was doing and showing them was wrong. But sometimes, saying "sorry" just isn't enough.

A lot of things happened in a short amount of time, all around the time that I finally hit my Rock Bottom. My oldest daughter, who I haven't talked about much in this story, had her problems too. She started taking various pills and drinking alcohol. She was under a lot of pressure, more than a teenage girl should have had to bear, but that doesn't excuse her bad choices. I won't go into that, and you'll come to understand why as we go through this part of my story.

Both of my daughters were from my first marriage. When their mother and I divorced, they continued to live with me, as I have already told you. I thought it was important that they stay in the home they had known, continue to go to the schools that they had always attended, and still be with the friends that they had grown up with. And I also wanted them to live with me. I wanted to be a part of their lives every day, not a few days a month. I didn't expect my marriage to end. I didn't plan for that or want that. But it did. Their mother also remarried and moved some distance away. For a while, it was just the three of us. My second marriage didn't happen right away. I really had the best intentions, wanted to be engaged in their lives, and be a good father. I think I managed that for a while, but then I ended up back on opiates, and everything started to go off the rails from that point.

As you already know, my second marriage was short lived and very toxic for everyone. My second wife, myself, my daughters. And things didn't really get better after that marriage ended. It was just the three of us again, but it was different. It had a distance in it that I didn't see at the time. Because I couldn't see through the drug haze I was living in. They were both teenagers by then and were starting to pull away, as all children do. It was just made much worse because I was an absent, drug addicted, bad father. And they were both starting to experiment with substances and alcohol. I didn't notice that they were pulling away or that they were starting to show the signs that I had shown at their age because, like I said, I was too high to notice.

My oldest daughter got her act together while my youngest daughter and I didn't. After I got my DUI, my oldest daughter really started to feel the pressure of our whole situation. I had already lost our home, as I told you about. They had moved in with my parents and were still going to school and trying to have "normal" lives. I was moving around, staying where I could, and getting deeper and deeper into my addiction. My oldest daughter decided that she had had enough and couldn't depend on me anymore. I still went to see them, still stayed in touch with them. Not everyday as I should have. She reached a point and made a decision that surprised me, hurt me, that I didn't see coming, but was, in retrospect, fair and shouldn't have been unexpected. She told me that she was going to file for emancipation. Her reasoning was that I wasn't dependable anymore, their mother was living in another city, and that it wasn't their grandparents', my parents', responsibility to be responsible for them. I wanted to argue with her, to tell her that I wouldn't let her do it. I tried to get her to change her mind. But she wouldn't. She told me that if she had to that she would take it in front of a judge and that I could try to defend my actions, my addiction, and my complete failure as a father. I knew that I couldn't defend anything that I had done. The intentions that I had when they were born, while they were growing up, had been surrendered to some really powerful and terrible drugs. I asked her why. She said that if I disappeared and didn't come back, that she wanted to be in a position to take custody of her sister, my youngest daughter, and make sure that she was safe and taken care of. That was more parental than I was being. It hurt to hear her words. But I couldn't argue that she was wrong. So, I consented and signed the paper. Giving her her freedom, her release from me and my bad choices. It didn't change much in our relationships. I was already pretty much gone, and they were already mostly on their own. I just accepted that they didn't really need me and kept digging the crater toward my Rock Bottom.

It wasn't long after that that my youngest daughter got into trouble, and you already know about that.

I started working on getting my life back together. My daughters and I moved into a house and started the repairs on the bridges that I'd attempted to destroy. I struggled, and they did too. Eventually, we had to move out of that house because it was going to be sold. My daughters moved back in with my parents, and I stayed there for a few weeks before moving back out into my vagabond, gypsy life. But at least this time I was doing it without drugs.

It was during this period that I met the woman who would become my third wife. We took time to get to know each other before making any rash decisions. She had been through a lot too, and wasn't in a hurry to make another mistake. We got to know each other through about six months. Her brother-in-law was able to help me get an interview where he worked. I told you how that went. It wasn't the best job I've ever had. But it was a start. After about six months, she and I found a mobile home that was available and moved in together. My oldest daughter had gotten married during this time, so she was already moving on with her life. She was 18 years old by then and deserved to have a chance to live her own life. My youngest daughter lived with us, got back into high school, started working, and we were all starting over together.

As I told you, things went sideways with my daughter, and she ended up going to live with her mother. You've already heard that part of the story. So, my then girlfriend and I continued to work on getting back to where we wanted to be.

Some time passed, and her son, my stepson, his wife, and their son decided to move back. They had been living in another state for several years. They had no place to go, no place to stay, and asked if they could come and stay with us "for a couple of weeks" while they got settled. We let them move in with the expectation that it would only be temporary. It wasn't as temporary as it was supposed to be.

The" couple of weeks" turned into several months. His wife got a job, but he wasn't able to find one. I helped him get a job where I was working, at the same place I told you about. The shovel and ditch place. His mother, my girlfriend still at the time, had already told me that he had a drinking problem. I didn't know how bad the problem was. He didn't want to go to work, he would sneak and drink beer on his lunch break and finally quit the job. His wife was still working, their son was in school, and they were still no closer to finding their own place as the day they moved in.

Many things happened that made that situation go really bad that I won't get into, because the details don't matter. Only this one. The night that everything came to a critical moment. They had been out. When they returned, he had been drinking heavily and was very intoxicated. He started saying things that he shouldn't have, and I'm not the type of person who will ignore that. It became a confrontation. I didn't want it to escalate into a physical confrontation, so I packed a bag and left for the night. I didn't want to get into a fight with him in front of his mother, his wife, or his son. It wouldn't have ended well, no matter how it turned out. I thought that maybe if I left, as the focus of his anger, that he would calm down, pass out, and sleep it off. The next day, I went to work. I spoke with my girlfriend, his mother, and the decision was made that the current arrangement couldn't continue. That they had to leave our home that day. Not a few days later, not the next day, but that day.

They packed the few belongings that they had and left. They stayed in a motel for a few days and were then able to find an apartment. My girlfriend and I were living together alone, again, and resumed our path of getting our lives together and getting to where we wanted to be.

I continued to work, she continued to work, and we both kept looking for better jobs, better opportunities, and did what we had to do to make our situation and our lives better. I found a better job with higher pay and benefits. She found another job as well. We found a better place to live and moved. It was just us and our dog. We were working, things were looking up for us, and we were closer to the life we wanted.

As I told you, my mom suffered from dementia. My parents had wanted us to get married for a long time. We had been living together and working on getting our lives straight for just over four years. My parents loved her, accepted her, and really wanted to see us happy and married. We had talked about getting married over the four years we had been together. We just hadn't ever been in any hurry.

We saw my mom's condition getting worse. Over the years we had been together, we had spent a lot of time at my parents' house. I helped my dad take care of his yard, helped him with whatever he needed help with. My wife would take my mom to town, to lunch, to a store, to get her nails or hair done. They came to know her and to love her deeply, and she them. She and my mom spent a lot of time together, and they talked about a lot of things. As my mom's condition worsened, she worried that I might lose focus and relapse, slip back under the spell of my demon. She asked my wife if she would promise to take care of me, to make sure that I didn't lose myself again. Even though I had been clean for a few years by then, had a good, stable job, and was doing right finally, she was still worried about me.

I'm going to get off track for just a moment. That hurt me deeply. She didn't hurt me by having that fear, or by voicing that concern. It hurt me that I had hurt her so badly that while everything else was slipping away from her, as happens to people who suffer that terrible disease of dementia, but that she still clearly remembered me at my worst. And she was still afraid that I could lose myself to addiction again. I had done that. I had caused that. And it hurt me that

I had hurt her so badly that she had never been able to shake that fear.

A few days later, my wife and I talked about that day, that statement, and her condition in general. And we decided that it was time that we got married. We were always on that path. We were just waiting for God to tell us it was time. Through my mother's words, He did. We wanted to get married, and we wanted to do it while my mom could still know that we did, that she could still be present enough that she knew that her request was being honored, that I would be "taken care of."

We got married a few weeks later. And we lost my mom 2 and a half months after we did. She was too sick to come to the wedding. But she knew, was able to understand, and was happy that we had. We took lots of pictures. We showed them to her and told her all about it. My youngest daughter would go and see her and sit beside her and show her the pictures over and over, many times.

My dad asked us to come and see them a month or so after we got married. He wanted to tell us something that he had been keeping to himself, but couldn't any longer. He had cancer. It was in his bones, his lungs, and his brain. He was scared. He knew that it was terminal and didn't know how much longer he could fight it. It was hard to hear. That was about six weeks before my mom passed away. He joined her 32 days after she left us.

It broke my heart that I had lost them. I meant what I said. They were the best people I ever knew. They had loved me from the moment I came into their lives and had never regretted having brought me there. No matter how badly I had disappointed them, no matter how badly I had messed up, or how deeply I had hurt them.

That was a short six weeks. I spent the night with my dad at the hospital two days before he died. I had a new job and couldn't stay the last night that he was with us. I went and started that job that day, went to see him at the hospital for what would be the last time.

I told you about getting my first and only DUI. I also got probation and fines. I had three years of probation and a few thousand dollars that I was supposed to pay. I moved around and ended up not completing all of the requirements of that probation. That was several years earlier. I was going to work for the second day at that new job when I was pulled over by the police. I was told that I had an outstanding warrant, and I was arrested. I didn't really comprehend at that time that it was because of the DUI and probation from years before.

Because I hadn't completed my probation, I was considered a fugitive from justice. Which meant that I wasn't going to get out any time soon. I was visited in jail that very day and told that my dad had passed away. I wasn't allowed to go to the hospital, even though they knew that he was not going to make it beyond that day. My wife was there, and my daughters. They told me that he was calling for me as he took his last breaths. That he was looking for me, wanted me there. But I wasn't. I couldn't be. Because I had made bad choices years before, and I had made more bad choices when I didn't make sure that I completed my probation completely and correctly.

The man that I respected above anyone else, that had loved me unconditionally, I had let down again. Because of the choices that I had made. I had been making better choices, doing things right, and was clean. But bad choices have a way of sticking around and rearing back up at the worst possible moments. And I had no one to blame but me. Again.

Because of the mess I had made by not following up and following through with my probation obligations, I was not granted bond and was not allowed to attend my father's funeral. I sat in a jail cell while he was buried. Because I had made bad choices. That was one of my consequences. That was one of the prices that I had to pay. And, again, I had no one else to blame but myself.

I was given one act of compassion, or pity, I'm not really sure why it was done. But I was taken to the funeral home before his funeral and given the opportunity to say goodbye. My wife was there. My daughters were there. My sister and her family were there. I was in jail house orange. My ankles were shackled, and my wrists. All connected by chains to a chain around my waist. I had to see my dad for the last time like that. It was devastating and one of the hardest things I've ever had to do.

My youngest daughter is highly emotional and started to get angry at the deputies who had brought me to the funeral home. She started telling them that it was wrong, that I shouldn't be in cuffs, that they should let me walk free. One of the deputies started to move toward her, started to say something. But he didn't get a chance.

I didn't give him a chance. I told her to sit down and shut up. I told her that she had no right or reason to be upset with those deputies. That those men were just doing their job, that they had been kind enough to bring me and give me an opportunity to say goodbye to my dad. I told her that she would treat them with the utmost respect and that she would apologize to them for her outburst. She did. I told her that I was in those shackles and in custody, going back to jail, because of things that I had done. No one was to blame but me. If she wanted to be mad at anyone, to be mad at me. The deputies were quite surprised by my reaction and words to her, everyone was. I'm not telling you this to get a pat on the back. I'm telling you because it happened. I couldn't allow disrespect in the presence of my dad. He wouldn't have allowed it, and I tried to honor him and handle it the way he would have. There were no further outbursts.

The visit was short, as it had to be. I took the opportunity, just before we left, to thank the deputies for bringing me and allowing me the opportunity to see him one last time. I also took a moment to tell my family that I accepted full responsibility for the situation that I was in. That I knew that it had been my actions that caused it. My choices. And I apologized again to them all. And to my dad.

I was taken back to jail and spent the next twenty-eight days there. Waiting to find out what was going to happen to me. I really did accept that whatever it was, that I deserved it and was solely to blame.

I was released, went back to work, determined to not let my mom and dad's memories, the promise that I had made to both of them, down. I wasn't going to let my wife down, or my daughters. And I wasn't going to break the promise I had made to myself and let me down.

A few months later, I had an epiphany while I was driving home from work. I had lost both of my parents in just a few short weeks. I had been in jail and wasn't there for my dad. I had had to resume my probation where I had left it unfinished years before. I had to pay several thousand dollars in attorney fees, and the remainder of my fines. My wife had suffered because of choices I made long before she met me. And she stood beside me through all of it anyway. What hit me on that drive home was that through all of that, I had not once thought about getting high. I hadn't even thought that I could have gotten, or wished I had, any drugs. I hadn't wanted any pills, any alcohol or any of the harder drugs that I had wasted so much of my life chasing. It surprised me, actually. It didn't make me want them at all. I told my wife about it when I got home. I told her that I could finally say I had beaten my demon, that I had beaten addiction.

I am proud of that. I know what I said before about pride. I didn't post it on social media. I didn't call everyone and sing my praises. I didn't break my arm patting myself on the back. But I was proud of that accomplishment. My wife was proud of me, too. And I think my parents would have been.

Life continued moving along, as it tends to do. My oldest daughter started pulling away, putting distance between us. She had told me more things that were still bothering her about the past, about things I had done when I was living in my addiction. I told her that I was sorry for all of it, and that I wished that I could change it. Apparently, she couldn't accept my apologies, couldn't forgive my past, and decided to pull herself away completely. I discovered one day that she had blocked me on social media. I tried to call her, tried to send her text messages, but I had been blocked there, too. I didn't want it to be that way, but, like I said before, everyone has to make their own choices about what they can or can't accept. It has been several years since she last spoke to me. I miss her, and I wish with all my heart that we could find a way to repair that bridge. I respect that she had a choice to make, and that she made it. But it doesn't make it any easier. And it certainly doesn't make it hurt any less.

I have been living a clean and sober life for many years. I don't have the same life that I had before I became an addict. Whatever that life would have been is forever lost. I am not proud of the time that I spend lost in addiction. But I made it through and came out stronger, with a clear mind and a new determination. I never considered myself a weak person, but compared to who I am today, I was. I had to be weak to allow myself to make the choices that led me to drug use and addiction. I had to make a new choice, a better choice. I had to choose to make better choices. Now I choose not to even consider taking opiate pain medication and would never consider anything illegal or illicit again. I told you the truth when I said that I tell doctors that I am an addict and that I can never be given or prescribed narcotic medications. As I said, I didn't go to a rehab. But that doesn't mean that you shouldn't. In fact, I recommend that you get professional help for yourself or anyone that you love and are trying to help. I didn't share my story with you so that you would praise me, think highly of me, or anything like that. I shared my story, my bad choices, my mistakes, and shortcomings so that you would see that I know who an addict is, what addicts do, and that it doesn't have to stay that way.

I get up every morning and go to work. I'm really not that different from anyone reading this. Like I said, I'm not rich, not a CEO of anything. I'm just a man that has made a lot of mistakes and learned a lot of things as I stumbled through my life. I hope that you have found something that can help you, no matter if you're the addict or the one that loves an addict, chart a path to a clean, sober, and peaceful life too.

As I'm writing this, telling you my story and showing you every skeleton I had hidden away, I am nearing the end of my thirteenth year clean. I am proud of that, too. I have, hopefully, a lot of life left to live. However much time I do have left, I know one thing without doubt. I will spend each minute of it clean and sober.

Chapter 22: What I Wish You Knew

One of the things that I have repeated many times is that I have never said "I used to be an addict." I have also said that I believe that anyone who does say that is wrong and is giving the wrong impression of what life after being trapped in addiction is. I have said that I believe that once you are an addict, you will always be an addict. I have had many people disagree and try to convince me that I am wrong. All have failed. The only time that anyone will ever be able to say that I used to be an addict is after I have taken my last breath. I believe that addiction stays with us for the rest of our lives. But that doesn't mean that you have to stay lost in your addiction.

I told you that I would explain what I meant, and I'm going to do that now. I am and will always be an addict. But I am not a drug user anymore. I made a choice many years ago to start making better choices, to start living the life I should have been living, and to make what time God has given me the best I can make it. And the only way to do that is to do it with a clear, sober mind.

I have had conversations with many people who were still trapped in their addiction or were struggling to start the journey to sobriety. I don't judge them. Only God can judge any of us. If they won't stop their substance abuse and self-destructive behavior, I tell them that they are making bad choices. I tell them that they need to open their eyes and start seeing themselves with honest eyes. I have had many people tell me that they knew that they needed to change, to make better choices, and wanted to be clean and sober. Most of them told me that they had tried and failed. They all had something in common. They didn't know how to stop.

I have also talked to parents and friends of addicts that were barely holding onto their sanity while they tried to understand why the person they loved was doing the things that they were. I have seen tears, have shed them myself, while we talked about the frustration, the helplessness of trying to help someone find their way out of their Hell. I have seen in their eyes the fear that they had lost the addict they loved and that they would never be able to help them, never see them be the person they could be. I have heard the desperation in their voices as they begged and pleaded, willing to give anything, even their own lives, if they could just get the addict to stop.

So, to the addict, what do I wish you knew? I wish you knew that there is a way, that there is hope. As long as we are breathing, as long as we are alive, there is a chance. A chance to start making better choices and to finally find a way to a clean, sober, meaningful, and peaceful life. It is not easy, but it is possible.

If you are an addict, there are people that still love you and still believe that you can make the choice to leave the substances, the self-destructive behaviors, the bad choices behind you. You might not believe that's true. But I would bet that it is. Even if you feel that everyone has abandoned you, because they refused to keep enabling you and aiding in your self-destruction, you need to know that they are just waiting for you to make the choice to get it right. You just have to take the first step. You have to do whatever it takes to get that journey started. Go to rehab, talk to a pastor, talk to a therapist, whatever it takes. You made a choice to start making bad choices. Now it's time to make a choice to make better ones. It's not too late. And I'm sure you will find that once you start on a path to sobriety, to better choices and a better life, that you won't be alone anymore. Not everyone will come back. Not everyone believes in you. But some, most probably, will come back if you make a serious, dedicated, and real attempt to get away from what is holding you down. It's not them. It's you. And you can change it. Only you, as I have said so many times. You will always be an addict. Just like I always will be. But you can make the choice to not use drugs anymore. Or to not drink alcohol anymore. To not gamble. To not do any of the self-destructive things that you have been doing. You will probably be in for the fight of your life. And it is a hard fight. You will feel pain, physical and emotional. You will doubt yourself. You will question yourself. Your addiction will try to hold you back, to not allow you to escape its grasp. Your mind will try to trick you into failure. But if you stand strong, if you believe that you can succeed, that you can beat your demon, you will reach the end of the battle as the victor. If you hold true to yourself, you will come out with scars that you will carry for the rest of your life. But you have to make a choice. The right choice this time.

If you are trying to understand, to help someone that you love that is an addict, you need to know that they can get out of their addiction. You need to know that they are not lost, that they don't have to spend the rest of their lives a prisoner of their bad choices. It is possible to get them back. And while they are the only ones who can make the choice to stop their bad behaviors and start making better choices, they will need you. They don't need you to enable them. They don't need you to push them into making different choices. They need you to believe that they can come back. I told you not to let yourself see things that aren't real, not to create false hope, and have unrealistic expectations. You have to protect yourself, but you have to be able to believe that it can happen. That they can make better choices and that they can be sober again. That they can leave the bad choices and self-destruction in the past and build a new, better life. When they are able to put all of it behind them, you need to understand that they won't be the same person they were before. They will be changed. I haven't met anyone who beat their addiction that wasn't different. I know this because I am not the same person I was. My daughter isn't the same person she was. And you won't be the same either. Just because you weren't under the influence of whatever demon was controlling the addict you love doesn't mean that you weren't suffering from their addiction too. You suffered in different ways. You suffered from the other side, but you have undoubtedly been changed too. You might not see the differences. And it's ok. You needed to change. You needed to learn to say "No." You needed to learn to be stronger. I won't say that you needed to feel guilty and worry about them every day. But because you went through that, you have changed and see things differently. You approach things differently, hopefully better than before.

And you need to know that their addiction was not your fault. Even if you were a parent or friend that showed them that bad behaviors were part of life, like I did. Even if you have skeletons in your closet, mistakes in your past. And yes, even if you offered it to them or even participated in their bad behaviors. It's not your fault that they made the choice to accept it and start down the path to destruction. I'm not saying that if you did those things that you weren't wrong. I was wrong to let my daughters see me do the things that I did. I'm saying that it's not your fault that they became an addict. It was their choice to make. A choice that they didn't know would affect not only them, but everyone who cared about them too.

I said before, and I will say again, that I don't think that anyone plans to become an addict. Nobody makes a conscious decision to get hooked on alcohol, or drugs, or anything else. But they do make the choice to try it the first time. Addiction is a terrible demon and a painful and lonely way to live a life. For the addict and for everyone that loves them.

I said that I don't judge people for being addicts. I don't let anyone judge me because I'm an addict. I'm not the person now that I was when I was lost to it. I am still an addict, that can never change. But I'm not a drug user anymore. I'm clean, and I choose to never let myself be that man again. So, I don't allow people to judge me now based on who I was then. You don't have to let anyone judge you either. If you are willing to make the choice to stop your bad and self-destructive behaviors, to make choices that make your life better, and you a better person, you don't have to let people treat you like the person you used to be. You don't have to fight them. You don't have to argue with them. I told you that some people won't come back into your life, and that some don't need to. You need to know that it's ok. Not everyone will believe in you, not everyone will be able to see past who you were before and what you did when you were in your addiction. Some won't be able to accept that you have changed, that you are making better choices, and are living a better life. Some will try to lure you back to the life you fought so hard to escape. You need to know that you don't need those people to move forward. It might hurt that some of your old friends aren't willing to be around anymore. Anyone who tries to get you to jeopardize your new life and choices doesn't need to be there, and you should not allow them to be. If you have made it, if you have found your way to a clean, sober, peaceful life, you should know that you deserve it and you shouldn't let anyone, or anything, take it away again.

If you are still struggling with addiction, if you can't find that first step to a better choice, you should know that you can. You need to know that there are people who love you and want to help you. That there are places you can go, professional people who can help you get started. And you also need to know, to remember, and to never forget, that only you can make the choice to fix yourself and start making better choices.

Writing this has been an experience. I didn't know when I started writing that it would lead me here. But here we are. I have said many times that I don't consider myself an expert, or better or smarter than anyone else. I have lived and I have learned, just like everyone else. I had one goal when I started writing ideas and notes on paper. That goal was to help my wife, and anyone else who was lost on either side of addiction, to understand. To understand the addict that they loved. To understand their feelings, frustrations, anger, and despair. It is my sincere hope that they found a little understanding, a little hope.

One more thing that I wish you knew is that it gets easier. If you're just getting started on your road to recovery and sobriety, it might seem like the fight, the struggle, will never end. You might fear that the voices trying to call you back, to lull you into giving up, will always be calling to you. I won't promise you that it will ever end completely. It hasn't for me, and I doubt that it ever has for anyone. But the calls will get weaker, they will stop being screams and become occasional whispers. The claws won't be able to grab you like they once did and are doubtless still trying to. You will never forget, and you don't need to. You need to always remember so you won't let yourself be fooled and coerced into bad choices again. I have been where you are. I have heard the calls. I have felt the push. I have had to fight the urge to give in and just let it take me back. Those voices promise you that if you just listen, if you just give in, just do what they tell you to do, that everything will be ok. You won't hurt anymore. Those voices lie. I want you to know that no matter what, if you stand strong and keep making the right choices, it does get easier.

I told you at the beginning that I would let you get to know me. That I would share my skeletons, my secrets, my mistakes. I also shared my success. It doesn't make me special that I was able to stop using drugs. It doesn't make me better than anyone else who has beaten addiction. Or that hasn't beaten it yet. It just makes me ME. It makes me who I am today.

What I wish you knew is that being an addict isn't the end. It doesn't have to be. I wish you knew, and now you do to some extent, what I know now. That life can be good again. That you don't have to stay a prisoner to your bad choices. That you can make better choices and find peace and happiness again.

That's what I wish you knew.

And if you're still wondering who I am, I'll tell you again.

I'm an addict.